SPIRITUAL POWER, HEALING HANDS

by

MALCOLM SMITH
with
ROBERT KRAJENKE

First published by 1st Books 10/27/05

ISBN: 1-4140-0136-3 (e)
ISBN: 1-4140-0137-1 (sc)

Printed in the United States of America
Bloomington, Indiana

This book is printed on acid-free paper.

Portions of this book originally appeared or were revised from HEALER! by Malcolm Smith with Jack Summers, (1988, MGOC Limited, Great Britain)

Be of good cheer. In truth, there are no incurable diseases!

Malcolm Smith

*****

EDGAR CAYCE: ADVICE FROM THE READINGS

(Q) *What steps should I now take to make my life a greater service for humanity?*

(A) Use thy abilities to heal, by the laying on of hands, by giving such suggestions that quiet the fears of those who are fearful and doubtful as to their relationships to the Creative Forces or God; thus bringing mental AND material health and joy to others. Reading 2620-2.

(Q) *Any advice regarding how to heal by laying on of hands?*

(A) As has been given here, praying with others and letting the vibrations from self pass through or into their bodies. Not taking ON the vibrations, but laying them all on Him. For He IS the healer, He IS life. He overcame death, hell and the grave. He overcame temptation. And in Him is peace, harmony, life.

With this accrediting, begin; not by proclaiming - for remember, as He oft gave, "Tell no man." Just be thyself, and thy trust in Him - and these bring the spirit of truth in thy labor of love for Him. Reading 2620-2.

ACKNOWLEDGEMENTS

My deepest thanks and appreciation to all those who have extended their hearts and hands, opened their homes, picked me up and delivered me to where I needed to go, booked my sessions, fed me, and made my work possible in the USA.

NEW YORK CITY The A.R.E. of New York Edgar Cayce Center volunteers who have helped make Malcolm Smith's healing sessions possible: Sylvia Chappell, Marie Clarke, Françoise Clarke, Katherine Korolenko, Richard Ottens, Paul and Rosalind Dorogoff, Lynne and Peter Miceli, Jaomic Olawale Kosoko, Edward "Ed" Everson, Leonard Cassara, Cliff Braverman, Catherine Outeiral, Joe Natale, Angela Climer, Michael Lopez, Lois Pitner, Brigitte Lippincott, Jerry Adorno, Sean Barden, Deb Keane, Amara Ward (we also thank Amara for proofreading/editing this revised version of this book), and to the memory of Alice Hall and Marie Crosby. **VIRGINIA BEACH, VIRGINIA** Art and Kathy Augsten, Jim and April Brown, Gay Hunt, Diana Clutton Taylor, Judith Van Cleave, and to the memory of "Buzz" Myers. **CHICAGO, ILLINOIS** Toni Romano, Diane Haggerstrom, Ruth and Don Niersbach, Dave and Nancy Rettger, Jim and Kathy Proszek, Iwona and Agnes Kurmika, Bob and Corrie Dieden, Pauline Browne, Sister Nancy, Ed Kent, Joyce Tumea, Leigh Garrison. **PEORIA, ILLINOIS** Victoria and Gregg Altorfer, Bob and Marilyn Dressden, Phil and Gary. **COLUMBUS, OHIO** Dan and Carol Borgnase, Sue and Wayne Keiser, Mr. and Mrs. Williams, Margaret Wilhelmy. **DAVENPORT, IOWA** to the memory of Jim Wright. **DENVER, COLORADO** Darlene and Bob Bodnar, Missy and Jeff Theesfeld. **DETROIT, MICHIGAN** Robert Krajenke, Lynne Browning-Krajenke, Heather and Meaghan Kangas, Louis Reeves, George Giffin, Bob Jones. **EL PASO, TEXAS** Richard and Victoria Brunch. **HOUSTON, TEXAS** Ed Jamail, Carl Bohannon, Robin Ricci, Terri Ricci, Alice Stacy, Lynne Marchitelli, MolleJo Murphy, Francis Gaza, Louie and Peter Harrison, Nancy & Marshall Webb. **NEW BRUNSWICK, TEXAS** Joann and Larry Aniol. **MILWAUKEE, WISCONSIN** Betty Riley, Kevin Reger. **NASHVILLE, TENNESSEE** John Thomas, Theresa and Roger Wing, Barbara Bramlett. **PHILADELPHIA, PENNSYLVANIA** Anita and Joseph Kosoy, Carol Garcia, Joan Reilly, Jean Taraborelli, Phyllis and Hans Vorhauer. **RENO, NEVADA** Mickie and Michael Moran. **NORTHERN CALIFORNIA** Grethe and Ted Tedrick, Jennifer Kreitzer, Sam Oshana, Kim Harvey, Linda Mahoney, Janet Rutherford, Lynne Jenichen, Carol Ross, Mandi Ross, LeRoy Williams, Rose Smith, Renee Ortiz, Kurt Albaugh, Jean Baxted, Chris Croskney, Brenda and Quentin Grady, Betty Callahan, Adair MacEachern, Iclea Halton, Jade Carol, Dalyn Wells. **SOUTHERN CALIFORNIA** Ron, Eileen, and Kirsten Johnson, Jeanine Alexander, Wilma Jackson, Linda King, Romualda "Rummy" Deksnys, Shannon Sweetmon, Nadine Sweetmon, Bette Macrae, Winona Crum, Barbara Cefalu. **SOUTHERN FLORIDA** Mary Ann Denn, Margot and Wayne Riekers, Lucy Smith. **KANSAS CITY, MISSOURI** Bill and Dot Kirklin, Ivah McNeall, Carol Sharp, Anthony Rizzo. **MONTREAL, CANADA** Bob Johnstone and Rosie D'Elia. And if I have inadvertently left anyone out, I do apologize; my thanks and appreciation go to you also.

DEDICATION

This book is dedicated to Karl Smith.

We will never forget you Karl. We talk of you often. You are always in our thoughts, in our hearts, and in our prayers. We love you and we miss you so very much.

Love from
Mum and Dad, Adele, Catherine, and Lauren

TABLE OF CONTENTS

FOREWORD

I pray for world peace and the healing of the planet. My life's purpose is to help people and the world by increasing humanity's awareness of God. The more aware we become of the reality of God as a totally accessible, loving, healing, caring Source, human behavior will improve. In the life of Jesus, we see God's love and caring made manifest to the lame, the blind and incurables through his healing miracles.

The evidence that God exists and is working healing miracles is all around us for anyone to see. Every day, the medical profession tells sick people that nothing more can be done for them. If they are lucky, they are advised to go home and live with their illness. If they are not so fortunate, they are pronounced incurable with no options but to go home and prepare to die.

My heart goes out to these people. I want them to know that there is always hope because God is unlimited in His power and mercy. Help can come to them in many ways, possibly through spiritual healers like myself.

To renew physical health is not the ultimate goal in Spiritual Healing. As the great American clairvoyant Edgar Cayce said, people need to be good <u>for</u> something. People need to have a reason, a purpose for being healed. For healing to be complete, there must be a change. If an individual continues living in the same manner that created the illness in the first place, how effective or long lasting can a healing be?

My purpose as a healer is to help people come closer to God. Through the gift of Spiritual Healing, I want them to experience that the love and healing energy we call God is as close to them as their own bones and marrow. My prayer is that this purpose is realized for you in the pages of this book.

MALCOLM SMITH, Yorkshire, England, May 2003

MY INTRODUCTION TO MALCOLM SMITH

By Judith Pennington

I drove for two hours, then took the train into New York City for an interview and session with Malcolm Smith, for three good reasons: first, because I felt a strong and inexplicable attraction to him, a sure sign of soul guidance; secondly, because his visits are sponsored by, among others, the A.R.E. (Edgar Cayce organization) of Houston and the A.R.E. Center of New York, which I trust implicitly; and thirdly, because I'd read stories of Smith's miraculous healings.

Walking the six blocks from Penn Station to the A.R.E. Center on 28th Street aggravated a long-standing problem with my back, but I didn't expect to be healed of it, as I'd had two profound healings during meditation, as well as periodic relief with self-Reiki and hands-on healers, none of which had lasted for more than a week.

I expected to feel heat in Smith's hands, but I encountered it immediately upon entering the center's office and meeting rooms. It wasn't the radiator, I decided, sitting down with volunteers to fold newsletters for the 20 minutes until my appointment.

Smith, a merry fellow with a pageboy haircut, emerged from behind a tall partition. "Where's the reporter from Time and Newsweek?" he joked. We shook hands and sat down in a small, partitioned space with a backless chair for me and another chair behind it for him. His slow, gentle introduction eased me into the session: the healing would last 25 minutes; he has an 80 percent success rate, with most of the healing coming on the third day; and he would need to place his hands here and there, was that okay?

Smith rested his hands lightly on my shoulders, and as he moved them from one spot to another, golden warmth spread through my body and I lost track of his semi-classical music and the rustle of papers in the next room. I prayed silently for the presence of divine helpers and the warmth intensified, with this healer playing my body like an instrument, lithely leaning me backward and from side to side. I was relaxed, supple, wondering vaguely where the pain had gone. ... Then suddenly the session was over and Smith was handing me a folded piece of cloth to place on my back at night and continue the healing, if needed. But where had the time gone?

I didn't voice my bewilderment, but somehow Smith, in walking me out, remarked that he doesn't remember the content of sessions either and is often surprised by what people recall that he said. He picked up a worn book of handwritten testimonials and leafed to a page with underlined writing. It read, "Malcolm asked me if I were aware of a terrorist attack coming to the U.S. from men who's hearts were full of evil. He said he felt it was very, very near, but I should not be frightened and that it would be good to have extra water and food on hand."

Smith predicted this two days before the terrorist attacks of September 11, 2001, and apparently the warning helped heal this client suffering from "terror that has consumed my life," the man wrote weeks later. Cured of his paralyzing fear in a single session, he spoke of Malcolm as an "earth angel" and of how, during his healing, he couldn't tell if he was sitting in the chair or floating above it.

I was hooked and read on while Malcolm worked on his next client. A woman wrote about crying for no apparent reason during her session and how a white light came over her that was so beautiful and full of love that she almost couldn't bear it; this light opened her "closed hard heart," she said.

A Jewish woman went to Smith for a healing of tinnitus (ringing in the ears), but Malcolm asked about the pain in her hand; she'd cut three fingers to the bone with a circular saw 25 years before, but didn't believe that he could help with this old, excruciatingly painful hand. After the healing, she felt relaxed and nauseous, and at home, vomited for hours; afterward, all of the pain in her hand was gone. Smith cured the tinnitus during her next session.

Other healings resolved multiple complaints in a single session. In one woman, a ruptured disk, frozen shoulder and emotional pain "healed below the surface, never to be seen (again). Words are insufficient," she wrote. An AIDS patient was thankful for the healing of a chronic pain in his shoulder, diminished asthma and an improved T-cell count enabling him to refuse "toxic medications."

One woman with aggressive breast cancer wrote that she needed no more surgery, after all. Another woman whose stitches wouldn't heal after a colostomy was suddenly healed except for the itching, she wrote ruefully. A man depressed about being jobless saw a vision of his mother during his healing and she told him not to worry; afterward, Malcolm said he'd seen her, too, and that his client would have a good job within two weeks and hear about it within two days. This is exactly what happened.

Next I came across an entry by a grateful mother writing about the healing of her 10-year-old daughter. The child suffered from low self-esteem and abysmal grades in school, but after a session with Smith, her test scores jumped from 50 to 100 percent. Her teacher wanted to know what had brought about such a dramatic change in Megan, whose attitude is now, "I can do it!"

I enjoyed reading of two dog healings that rule out the power of suggestion in these cases at the very least. An 8-year-old Border collie's health had begun to fail, leaving him with a dull coat, constant scratching, weakness causing him to fall down stairs, and what seemed to be depression. After one visit and three nights of having the folded cloth held against his body, King was cured, healthy and happy again. So was a 12-year-old poodle brought to Smith for congestive heart failure, kidney failure and a yearlong illness. After four visits, Ginger rallied and is the "longest living dog" known to her veterinarian.

Now I not only wanted — but also needed — to know more about this healer and his gift. It was my good fortune to receive a healing from Smith, as several good things have since happened to me. For one thing, the increased energy in my body has enlivened my meditations and my ability to see visions and derive their meanings. This is remarkable for me, and I've learned that to cure my back pain permanently, I must cure the underlying cause: re-injury due to busy haste and a lack of consideration for my body's basic needs.

I've also noticed that at the end of my meditations, during my healing prayers for others, the stirring of energy in my hands, feet and other spiritual centers is much stronger than before. Yesterday, my four-year-old grandson fell down five wooden steps and landed on the bones of his eye socket. We share "the healing energy" often, as we call it, but this time his intense pain disappeared almost instantly, and, as he snuggled against me, he was noticeably reluctant to get up and move away. I suspect that he felt something wonderful, as I sensed a subtle difference in and a peculiar air about him. There's been no bruising at all, so it seems that I got exactly what I needed from Malcolm: healing energy and the backbone to use it.

We always get what we need, don't we? If only we ask and follow our guidance to it.

*Judith Pennington is a spiritual teacher and educator. For more about her, visit her website at **www.eaglewings.com**.*

I DREAM OF OPRAH

By Malcolm Smith

The Bible tells us that God speaks to us through visions and dreams. Two weeks after I completed the first draft of my manuscript, I had a vivid, spiritual dream. In the dream I am sitting on a bench in a small park. In front of me, a small road continues through the park. Where I am sitting, the sun is shining, and I hear birds singing. The lawns are well manicured, with a few trees here and there, and park benches scattered about. I know I am in America because, at the edge of the park, beyond the trees I can see New York's Empire State Building on my right and the Chicago Sears Tower on my left.

On the other side of the road, there are dark clouds and it is raining. Many poor, unfortunate souls are seated on the benches, looking forlorn and desolate. They all look 'down and out.' Some are standing; others are laying or sitting on the lawns.

On my side of the road, it is warm and sunny. On their side of the park, the rain comes down heavily. As I pondered why this should be, a white stretch limo with smoked glass windows pulls up right in front of me. The driver is a black female wearing a white gown and a mortarboard hat, the kind you see at graduations. She gets out of the limo and stares at the homeless people, and then turns around to face me, and says, "Can you help these people?" It was Oprah Winfrey! "I can't help them," I answer. "I don't have any money to help them."

She goes back to the car and taps gently on the tinted glass window. The window opens a few inches and Oprah has a few words with someone inside. I couldn't see to whom she was talking or hear what was said. The window goes up and Oprah comes back to me. "Just give them your book" she says, and gets back in the limo and drives down a road that circles through the park. Soon she is back. I wonder what does she mean "give them the book." As I am thinking this, Oprah gets out of the limo and looks over at the people in the park. They are still there, and I am still sitting on the bench. She turns to me, and rather annoyed, she says, "Why haven't you helped these people?" "I don't have any money," I reply sheepishly. Oprah goes back to the limo, taps on the window, and has a brief conversation with the passenger behind the dark glass window. Then she faces me and says very emphatically, "Just give them your book!" She gets in the limo, drives off and circles the park once more.

I look down. All around me are stacks of my book. "Well, maybe I can sell them, and use the money to help these people," I think. In a moment the limo is back. Oprah gets out and looks over the park. It is still cloudy and dark on that side of the park, but with some shafts of sunlight coming through. And there are fewer people now. There were about fifty, now there are maybe thirty or less. Some are sitting in the sunlight.

She is very pleased and turns to me. "You helped them," she says. "Well done."

"Why are there still people sitting in the rain?"

"We can all help somebody, but we can't help everybody." With that, Oprah removes her cap and throws it to me.

"What's this for?"

"Don't you know?" she says and starts to drive away. As the limo drives past me, the back window comes down a few inches and I glimpse the person in the back seat. It is Jesus! He smiles, and the window goes back up. And I awake.

The dream was very vivid and its impact has stayed with me through the years. The impact of Oprah's positive philosophy and spirit has inspired and "awakened" millions of people throughout the planet, including me. But Oprah is only a messenger taking her directions from the man in the back seat, the Lord Himself. I believe this dream is showing me that the healing spirit of love and hope manifested in Jesus is encouraging me to share my story with you, not because I'm someone special, but because I am just a guy in the park who stands on the sunny side, a person just like you who has a story to tell that may take some of the rain and darkness from your life.

WHAT IS SPIRITUAL HEALING?

Of all the forms of healing, Spiritual Healing is perhaps the oldest — and the most controversial. Ancient pictographs on rocks and cave walls throughout the planet show scenes of what appear to be shaman healers channeling energy to distressed persons, while above them are figures that appear to be spirit guides or angels. The pictographs date back thousands, perhaps tens of thousands, of years, and yet, in terms of Spiritual Healing, the scene could just as easily be taking place today.

Spiritual Healing involves a healer and the person receiving the energy. The healing is from God, and the energy is administered through spiritual guides, angels, or spirit doctors. The spiritual healer's belief and reliance upon the spirit realm in the healing process makes Spiritual Healing controversial and unacceptable to many. Spiritual healers believe the healing energy has its source in Spirit, not the earth, and that the healer is only an intermediary, or channel through which the guides work. I like to say that I am only an innocent bystander in the process.

The primary purpose of Spiritual Healing is not to heal the body. This is only a secondary objective. *The primary purpose is to touch the soul!* Edgar Cayce, regarded as the father of the holistic health movement and the greatest medical clairvoyant of the 20th Century, stated that his psychic work was not to aid physicians with diagnostic insights or bring about miraculous cures, but to help open people's minds to the truth about the spiritual world. His healing work was essentially a spiritual mission.

If the soul or spirit of the person is not reached by the healing energy, then any physical improvement will only be temporary. Frequently, people experience a removal of symptoms, only to have the symptoms return. Great healers, such as Harry Edwards in England and Kathryn Kuhlman, Oral Roberts and Olga and Ambrose Worral in America, were often mistakenly accused of fraud or being charlatans when people who received dramatic healings at their services had their symptoms return within a few days or weeks. If symptoms return, it doesn't mean the healing has failed, only that the cause of the illness is resisting the healing energy.

Even when Spiritual Healing appears to be successful, symptoms often return. It's part of the process. The cause must be completely overcome. The healing energy and the source of the disease war with each other. In the beginning, the cause will win the battles, but in the end, if the person sticks with the process, the healing energy will win the war. In my work, 80% of the people who come for Spiritual Healing will receive help in some form. Either they will be completely healed from head to toe, or there will be a degree of improvement, but not 100%. In a small percentage of cases, an individual is instantaneously healed. Another small percent will receive no discernible help at all. If nothing happens after three or four sessions, you can be reasonably sure nothing much will happen on the fifth or sixth. Spiritual Healing is not for everyone.

All too often in our busy lives our spiritual self is neglected, and the spirit within us suffers. It can grow weak, and our connection to the Divine becomes blocked, closed, or compromised. All successful Spiritual Healings testify to a higher power, and, therefore, awareness must arise within the individual of a need for a new code of moral and spiritual values to replace those that have them "bogged down" in material cares and woes. Unless the soul is touched and the mind of the physical being opens to the healing energy of its spiritual source, the healing will fail.

Spiritual Healing operates according to law. It follows a distinct, discernible pattern. It's not faith healing. It's not a shortcut. You don't even have to believe in it. Spiritual Healing works for babies, animals, people in comas, atheists and agnostics. Babies and animals don't have faith, and still it works. If it's going to work for you, it will work within the universal laws that govern it, regardless of your belief.

Spiritual Healing is a process and continues over time. As awareness of our spiritual connection becomes more conscious and developed, inevitably the cares, worries, fears and concerns that trouble the mind and foster disease lessen and fade until they are totally gone.

Be of good cheer. In truth, there are no incurable diseases!

Now, this is my story.

*****

When they arrived, they were speechless. They both recognized my house with its manicured lawn and ivy on the walls as the very house that Dean had seen two years before in his dream. (page 97)

CHAPTER ONE

EARLY MEMORIES

"How long have you been a healer?"

I am repeatedly asked that question. Most often I say, "Oh, since 1979." But the power of hindsight is very strong. Looking back, several instances make me wonder.

I was only ten years old, when my father woke me around 3:30 a.m. one morning.

"Your Gran has taken ill. I need you to sit with her and hold her hand until I get back. I'm going to fetch Aunt Dorothy."

I knew he would be gone for at least half an hour. Next to my Dad, I loved Grandma Smith dearly. She had been mother and grandmother to me since my own mother died when I was seven days old. Now my beloved Gran was delirious, gasping for breath and writhing in great agony. I went to her bed and gripped her gnarled old hand.

"Arthur? Arthur, is that you?" she moaned. She kept asking if I were Arthur - my late grandfather.

"No, it's me, Malc."

As I held her hand her pain spasms seemed to reduce. Then, suddenly, she stopped trembling and the heavy sweat that had been pouring from her disappeared. She was quiet and calm. Her eyes closed. A sudden terror overtook me. I had let her die! What would Dad say?

"Please, please God, don't let her die!" I cried. I ran into my bedroom full of fear and threw myself on the bed. I prayed harder than I had ever prayed in all my ten years.

A few minutes later, the front door opened. Dad was back with Aunt Dorothy. They started up the stairs. I slipped from my bed, tears streaming down my face.

"It's not my fault, Dad. It's not my fault," I pleaded.

"What are you saying, son?"

"Gran's dead."

Dad and Aunt Dorothy rushed into Gran's room. I waited outside and listened at the door.

"Ah, the fever's broken." Aunt Dorothy said. "Just let her sleep."

"Thank God." Dad sounded tired.

Grannie Smith slept soundly for twelve more hours, and when she woke up, the crisis was over. She was back to normal. Through all those hours I did not - could not - imagine her swift recovery was from the healing energy passing through me. Yet, looking back, her recovery started the moment I took her hand and prayed to God not to let her die. Did I have the power then, all those years ago? Other pieces of evidence suggest I had powers, even then.

A year later, on my way home from a Sunday school at the local church, an overwhelming urge to know the time came over me. It was a compulsion I couldn't deny. I ran up to a man walking toward me.

"What time is it?" I asked.

The man pulled his sleeve back and showed me his watch. It was exactly 10:55 a.m. A strange feeling of concern ran through me and stayed with me the rest of the day. At teatime a relative from another village arrived to tell us of a death in the family. A great aunt, a favorite of mine, had died that morning - at 10:55 a.m.

Many years later, during a period of unemployment, I had my first encounter with a clairvoyant, a medium named Martha Dyson. I have met, or read about many mediums and psychics since, each having, or claiming special gifts. Not until I learned about Edgar Cayce, did I find any that compared with Martha.

On one particular morning, Mary Beth, a cousin of mine, insisted that I take her to see Martha. I had no money, and there was no gas in my tank. Mary Beth loaned me two dollars for fuel, and we reached Martha's house late in the morning. Martha greeted us and took us to her little kitchen. I sat by the coal fire, enjoying its warmth while Mary Beth had her reading in the next room. When they came back into the kitchen, I stood up, ready to go.

"Would you like a reading, love?" asked Martha.

"Er, no thanks, I don't have any money and I've somewhere to go." It was a white lie, and a flush of shame warmed my cheeks as I told it.

She leaned toward me. "You don't have anywhere else to go, son. Now come along, it won't hurt you." Martha led me into the small front room.

"I sense some connection with the sea coming soon. I see you surrounded by machinery." A few weeks earlier, I had submitted a written application to the Merchant Navy, and as yet had received no reply. Before that, I had been turned down.

Her next words scared and puzzled me.

"I can see a lady standing by your side. She says that she is your mother and that both she and the baby are very happy."

"It couldn't be my Mum," I answered. "My mother died in childbirth. I was her only child."

Martha went quiet for a few moments. Her head tilted, as though she was listening to someone.

"She tells me that it is your birthday in a few days time!" I looked around to see what Martha was seeing. There was nothing.

"It's true, but it won't be my Mum, not with a baby," I protested.

"Who is Alice?"

"That's my mother's name!"

"Then I'm telling you this lady is your mother and she took a baby over to the other side when she passed."

I knew very little about my mother and absolutely nothing about any details of her death. My Dad was devastated by my mother's death. It was so painful for him that Gran and I were never allowed to talk about her.

3

Her head tilted, and she went silent again. "She tells me that the truth about this baby will be given to you sometime in the next three weeks."

I wasn't going to argue with her. She was wrong, and that was it. I bid her good day and asked how much I owed her.

"Nothing," she answered. "You had to borrow money to come here today. Come back and give me something when you are rich."

Martha took us to the door. I walked a few steps when she called me back.

"By the way, tell your Dad that if he doesn't go to the doctor with that leg of his, he'll lose it!"

How on earth could she know about my Dad's problem with his leg? I wanted to dismiss it as some kind of 'con' - except I knew that Mary Beth had never told Martha anything about me.

Dad went to the doctor and discovered he had a serious infection in his leg.

"Had you waited any longer," the doctor said, "gangrene might have set in."

Four weeks after my reading from Martha, I was accepted into the Merchant Navy! After a few short weeks of training in Liverpool, I shipped out on the mighty 'Queen Elizabeth,' working below deck in the engine room as a bilge diver. Indeed I was surrounded by machinery, just as Martha had foreseen.

A week before I was due to ship out, I dropped in on an old friend of my Gran's. We were enjoying a long chat, when suddenly she paused and looked at me intently.

"I wonder if the other one would have grown up like you?"

"What other one?" I gasped.

"Your twin brother, Malc. Don't tell me you don't know about him!"

A cold chill surged down my spine.

"A twin? I don't have a twin brother."

"You were the first born of twins," she answered, slightly amazed by my ignorance. "Your brother was stillborn. No one ever told you?"

"No, ma'am. It's never been mentioned, until now. My Dad couldn't bear for us to speak of anything to do with her passing."

But how could Martha, a total stranger, know what was unknown to me for twenty-one years? It puzzled me deeply, and created a sense of awe. Although it would be another twelve years before the torch of Spiritualism burned bright in me, that day the flame was kindled.

HOW IT ALL BEGAN

I believe everyone has the power to heal. It's a gift from God, given to every soul. We are born with the gift, but how we use it, how we develop it, is our own choice to make.

My journey as a healer began simply enough. One evening in early February of 1979, my wife Kathleen and I decided to visit my cousin Betty Wilson. Betty lived in a flat a few miles away in South Elmsall. She had become involved with a local Spiritualist Church where she was developing her gift of clairvoyance. I was curious to know how she was progressing. When we arrived, Betty was enjoying a cup of tea with a friend, a well-known psychic in her village. No sooner were introductions made than this woman looked straight at me and wagged a finger in my face.

"Young man, do you know you have healing hands?"

I did not. In fact, I had to ask her, with some embarrassment, what she meant by "healing hands."

"You can put your hands on people and make them better."

My response was a self-conscious, barely concealed snigger.

"You don't believe me, do you?" she accused. "Well, I'll tell you this, lad. The pain from your wife's kidney infection will return in a few days. When it does, put your hands over the area of pain and see what happens." She looked me in the eye, and nodded her head slightly. "I'll tell you something else, as well, one day you will go out healing the sick, and become world famous!"

World famous? The woman was mentally unbalanced! I was a thirty-three-year-old coal miner with a tenth grade education. I'd been married eleven years and had three young children, seven-year-old Adele, five-year-old Karl, and one-year-old Catherine. While I had settled down considerably, I had previously been something of a hell-raiser as well.

It was true, Kath did have a chronic kidney condition, and she had been plagued with it since giving birth to Catherine, our youngest, but just the week before, the hospital had pronounced her totally cured. I glanced at my cousin for her reaction.

"Don't laugh, Malc. It will come true," she insisted, laying a reassuring hand on my arm.

Two days later, Kath experienced yet another bout of kidney infection. The pain in her back grew steadily worse all day. By six o'clock, the pain was acute. I felt helpless as I watched the tears streaming down her face. I knew that the pain could last for twenty-four hours or more before it eventually subsided on its own. I also knew that these attacks were becoming more frequent, and that each was worse than the last.

Sitting with her, trying to give her whatever comfort I could, the words from my cousin's friend kept flashing through my mind - "You have healing hands. Go out and heal the sick!"

"Please, let it be true!" I prayed. I wanted desperately to help Kathleen. I went into the kitchen and returned carrying a stool.

"Kath! Come and sit on this stool. I'm going to put my hands on your back." I helped her from the settee onto the stool, and then placed my hands over the kidney area of her back.

"Your hands! They feel red-hot!" Kath cried out. "The whole of my back is burning! What's happening, Malc?"

"I don't know, Kath. I don't feel anything coming from my hands." I had no answer.

In less than a minute, Kath's pains started to subside. In no time at all, they completely vanished. To this day they have never returned.

I was more stunned than surprised. How could an ordinary person like me put his hands on someone and take away pain and suffering? Was it a coincidence, the result of self-suggestion, or simply a placebo?

Three days later I had a chance to test it out again. My five-year-old son Karl developed conjunctivitis, a painful inflammation of the eyes. Kath took him that evening for an examination. The doctor looked him over and said it would take about two weeks to clear up. He prescribed a course of antibiotics and eye drops. By the time Kath left the doctor's office, the pharmacy was closed. She was unable to get the prescription filled that night.

Karl wasn't as upset as he might have been. He knew his inflamed and swollen eyes meant no school tomorrow, and possibly not for a week or more. Even so, as we sat around the television watching our favorite soap opera, his tears began to flow.

"Dad, my eyes are stinging and it hurts. Dad, put your hands on my eyes and make them better like you made my mam better," he pleaded. It hadn't even entered my head that I should try to heal him.

"Try it," Kath said, cradling her only son on her knee. I went over and placed my hands over his eyes.

"Your hands are hot, Dad!" Karl exclaimed. Again, I felt nothing coming through my touch. I held my hands over his eyes for three or four minutes, hoping for a miracle, but his eyes remained red and watery.

"Do they feel any better?"

"No, Dad, they still hurt, but you've made me feel all hot and I feel ever so tired."

His reply was disappointing. Nagging self-doubt chewed to shreds what confidence I had in my newfound power. I dropped my hands to my side. Was it only a coincidence that Kath's kidney pains disappeared? I suddenly felt very tired. It had been a hard day in the mine. We put Karl to bed, and I called it a night as well.

The next morning, I woke up early and decided to treat Kath to a luxury usually restricted to Mother's Day — breakfast in bed. I was frying eggs in the pan, when I heard a small sound behind me. It was Karl, pajama-clad and tousle-haired, rubbing both eyes with the palms of his hands. When he took his hands away, two clear, baby blue eyes gazed up at me. I was dumbstruck. There were no signs of inflammation or watering.

"How do your eyes feel?" I managed to ask.

"They're okay," he said, almost as if the healing was something he took for granted, "but do I have to go to school today, Dad?"

I grabbed him in my arms and rushed upstairs and ran into the bedroom.

"Kath! Kath, you're not going to believe this!" I turned to show her Karl's face.

"Oh my God," she gasped, equally astounded as I. Our celebration was broken by the smell of burning eggs downstairs.

"Damn," I snorted, "I wanted to surprise you with a special treat today."

"I've been served an even better surprise," she answered, snuggling her son.

VISITS FROM A POLTERGEIST

Even with this success I couldn't bring myself to tell anyone outside my immediate family circle that I had this gift. Life in a small Yorkshire mining village has its drawbacks. I could imagine the reaction of my neighbors if I told them that I recently acquired the gift of healing. The Fundamentalists would think I was possessed by the devil. My cousins might call me crazy. Miners are very macho, and I feared their ridicule and laughter. I could only guess what would happen if I announced "Mates, let me put me hands on you. I can heal what ails you with me touch." They'd run me out of town — or worse. So, for the next two years, I restricted my healing to my wife and children, limiting the power to headaches, tummy upsets and other minor ailments.

To be honest, I hadn't a clue as to just how powerful this healing force was or is. Or if it was even real. My education was just beginning.

In August of that same year, my daughter Adele caught a heavy chest cold, which eventually turned to bronchitis. One night, just before bedtime, I gave her healing, hoping she might get some ease and have a good night's sleep. The next morning, there was some improvement, but from the wheezing sounds she was making, it was obvious that she was far from healed. But what came next was greatly disturbing and equally hard to comprehend.

"Dad! I woke up in the night and there was a man standing by the side of my bed."

"You must have been dreaming about Grandad again," I said reassuringly. My father, who had lived just two doors away and whom our kids worshipped, had died the previous October. Since then, he had appeared quite often to Karl and Adele in their dreams.

"No, Dad," Adele insisted. "It wasn't a dream. I woke up and this man was standing there." Adele described him as very tall and with a beard. He bent over her, she said, and put his hands on her chest. They were red hot.

"When he saw I was looking at him, he smiled at me and I went back to sleep. I wasn't frightened, Dad, he was ever so kind!"

This was the first appearance of a being that, over the coming years, many other people who received healing would see. I never reveal any details about this figure, other than people say that he is tall with a beard and that 'He is ever so kind.' But in all the sightings and encounters involving him, the descriptions of how he is dressed, the type of jewelry he wears and other details are consistent. Adele was the first to see him, and in over 24 years of healing, he's been seen 12 or 13 times by different people, and, in all cases, the details, even down to a specific piece of jewelry he wears, have been the same. He usually comes when they are in a deep sleep state in the middle of the night. So, on occasion, people wake from their sleep, see him and are frightened.

While his smile was reassuring to Adele, and she felt no fear of him, his appearance was followed by visitations from a poltergeist. Strange happenings began to rock the house. For the next three months, even on calm, windless days, bedroom doors started to slam shut and fly open of their own accord. The lights in the house and the water taps turned on and off. Once, we came home from a family outing to the movies to discover all the faucets running and the bathtub overflowing. Small articles like rings or watches that were kept in regular, appointed places - including a telephone directory - disappeared, only to turn up again a couple of days later in the same places they were always kept. One time, as we sat watching television, a loud bang shot out from the cupboard in the kitchen. A heat resistant Pyrex dish had shattered into small pieces, yet it had not fallen, neither had anything else fallen on it. Another morning, as Kath changed baby Catherine's diaper, a heavy wooden wall plaque rose off the two nails supporting it, hovered in mid-air for a couple of seconds, then crashed to the ground. No damage was done, but it severely frightened Kath. Adele, on the other hand, who was also in the room, thought it was hilarious. And then, in the early hours of the morning, came the most eerie part of all. We could hear children on the landing. Sometimes they were laughing, other times weeping. It was all quite strange and disconcerting.

It came to a head one Wednesday night in October. Kath and I had gone to bed around eleven o'clock. We had barely slipped under the covers when we heard heavy footsteps starting up the stairs and a noise as if someone with a stick was tapping on the staircase wall. When the footsteps reached the top of the landing, they started down the steps, tapping continuously on the wall. Kath clung to me tightly for the next five minutes.

"For God's sake, go and see what it is!" she said finally.

I was in no mood to be a hero.

"You b-b-bloody well go and see what it is," I stammered. "You're nearest the door!"

In the end, Kath prevailed. I grabbed a baseball bat and tiptoed toward the door and waited. When the footsteps reached the landing, I rushed out like a Samurai warrior, my war club raised high above my head, hoping to get at least one blow in. No one was there.

I turned on the landing light. Nothing. Satisfied, I turned to switch off the light only to feel a bone chilling icy presence directly in front of me. In a flash, I was back in bed with the covers up to my chin.

"You've left the light on, love!" said the wife in an irritatingly calm voice.

"If you want the light off, switch it off yourself!" I snapped like a true coward. She never did.

This was a turning point for me. In addition to exposing a not very nice side of my nature, I knew something had to be done! Things could only get worse!

DISCOVERING SPIRITUALISM

The following morning, I telephoned a couple of friends who periodically visited a Spiritualist Church in the small mining town of South Elmsall, where my cousin Betty lived. A stranger to Spiritualism, I found some of their beliefs about life after death, spirit communication and medium-ship hard to accept. However, at this point, if they told me King Kong had materialized wearing a crash helmet and goggles, I was ready to believe.

"The next time you go to church," I said, "I'd like to go with you."

"Sure! There's a service tonight. We'll be glad to take you along."

I had no idea what was coming. I imagined a grubby, dimly lit place with cobwebs and bats flying and people with hoods over their heads doing strange rituals. It was quite the opposite. The church was small, very clean, well lit and quite homey. Twenty or thirty chairs were set out in a circle, and no bats were flapping about. The people appeared quite normal.

We took our seats and the little church filled rapidly.

"When do they switch the lights off?" I asked eagerly.

"Shish! They don't turn them off," my friend whispered back.

Hymns were sung, prayers were said, and the service got underway. The mediums delivered messages to the congregation. None were given to me, however, but I found it extremely interesting. I discovered the church held weekly healing services, with the 'laying on of hands' — and a new class for healers was forming that evening. I had never heard of anything like this before, and was very relieved to know I wasn't the only one doing what they called "contact healing." Other forms of healing were taught, too. I would soon learn about them, and begin practicing. But for now, I was told to 'sit in' and watch the healers at work. Questions could be asked after the healing service was over.

The most important thing that night occurred after the service was over. My hopes for the evening were that I could find a medium from the church who could rid me of my unwelcome visitors. I asked around, and an old lady, a seer, said she would consult with Ariel, her guide and try to get an answer for my problem. She went into another room to meditate. Ten minutes later, she reappeared with a message from her guide.

"There will be no more poltergeists," she announced. "It will stop today, its job is done."

I was incredulous. "What do you mean, 'its job is done?'"

"Ariel says the purpose for the poltergeist was to get you to this church, and now that you're here, it has done its work."

"But why?" I asked. "What for?"

Ariel wouldn't reveal the reason. Apparently, on the other side, they weren't pleased with my choice to keep my talent under a bushel, so to speak. So they decided to give me a kick in the pants. There is an old saying that whom the gods cannot lead, they shove — and they don't always tell you their reasons. Ariel was right. From that day forward, all the supernatural activity in our house ceased.

Looking back, I am convinced that these disturbances were deliberately caused to direct me to a Spiritualist Church. The Spiritualist Movement nurtured my healing gift and provided the information I needed to stop worrying what others might think or say about me and move forward in my ministry.

A RESTLESS APPRENTICE

The church at Elmsall, like most Spiritualist Churches, insisted on a probation period of six months before would-be healers are allowed to do the laying on of hands. During this initial probation period, the apprentice healer is not allowed to touch any of the people receiving healing. This restriction weeds out the really interested from the merely curious. After six months, a group of 13 or 14 will dwindle down to three or less. We were told, as healers, we must have patience and so must the client. Instant miracles are rare. If a healer doesn't have the patience to see the process through, after two or three sessions he or she tends to drop out and move on. Our teacher also explained about guides and spirit doctors, and how spirit guides actually select and develop the spiritual healers they work through. "God is the source of the power," she said, "the guides administer the power, and the healer is the conduit for the healing energy." In other words, the healer is a plug that fits into a socket so the energy can flow from the Source to where it's directed.

I confess it wasn't long before I grew bored with 'sitting in.' There was nothing to hold my interest. It was always the same half dozen elderly ladies suffering with arthritis, headaches and stiff joints. Although they didn't seem to get worse, they never seemed to improve either. After six weeks I decided to give it up.

Two weeks later in a Spiritualist Church in Normanton, three miles west of Pontefract, I sat next to an elderly gentleman named Tommy Smith (no relation). With his shaven head and potbelly, he reminded me of a Buddhist monk. Mild, well-mannered, soft-spoken and capable of extraordinary kindness, Tommy was a gentleman in every sense of the word. Over a cup of tea I told him about my experiences, including my frustration with not being able to do any healing at the South Elmsall church.

"Why don't you come over and help us out here at Normanton," suggested Tommy in his quiet Yorkshire accent.

"Will I have to sit and watch for six months before I'm allowed to do any healing?"

"Be here for 6 p.m. this Saturday," Tommy smiled and gave me a cheerful wink.

I felt a surge of excitement as I visualized myself standing side by side with established healers, relieving a line of desperate souls from pain and suffering — a modern day Ivanhoe, the people's champion!

Saturday couldn't come fast enough. I was half an hour early. The church was open and Tommy was sitting in quiet meditation at the front of the building. I joined him. Forty-five minutes ticked by. Tommy was still sitting with his eyes closed. I checked my watch and glanced at the church door.

"Tommy where is the rest of the healing team?"

"We are it," Tommy replied without opening his eyes.

"But Tommy, how on earth are we going to get through all the people who come for healing?" I felt almost panic stricken.

"With humility and simplicity," he replied.

Ten more minutes passed before the church door rattled open. Two elderly ladies shuffled in. They took their seats, and we gave them healing.

"Would you please make us a cup of tea," Tommy asked one of the ladies.

"Tommy! We can't have a tea break yet," I protested, "What about the rest of the people who want healing! We can't have them waiting, can we?"

Tommy smiled and put his arm around my shoulder. "Son, this church is like a lighthouse, and we are its keepers. If we can shine a glimmer of light into the life of just one person whose life is darkened by pain, or suffering, then we have done well."

The two elderly ladies were the only desperate souls in need of our services that night. The weeks came and went. Sometimes as many as four people came for healing, always for their backaches, stiff joints and headaches. Sometimes there was improvement in their conditions, sometimes not, and mostly it was the same people who kept returning. I was sure they were more interested in socializing over tea and biscuits than in receiving healing. By March 1980, it was down to one, and I seriously doubted that Spiritual Healing was my calling. I felt ready to end my brief career as a spiritual healer.

DISCOVERING HARRY EDWARDS

One Saturday evening, I decided this would be my last healing service. As Tommy was passing healing power to the last sufferer in the 'queue of desperate souls' needing our services, I became aware of a beautiful, warm feeling on the back of my neck. I turned to see what was causing the heat. The sun's rays were passing through the windows directly behind me. A single shaft of sunlight focused itself on Tommy and his client and moved slowly across the church, finally resting on a small collection of books standing on a shelf at the end of the room. One book in particular seemed to be illuminated; or maybe it was just my imagination, but it appeared to glow.

I waited until Tommy finished the closing prayer, and then went over to investigate. I pulled the book from the shelf. The cover picture showed a kind, but strong face of a gentleman with white hair. It was the author, Harry Edwards. The book title read *Spirit Healing*.

"Tommy, who is Harry Edwards?" I asked, holding up the book. Tommy's face lit up with a smile of recognition.

"Oh, Malc, Harry Edwards is no doubt the greatest healer since Jesus Christ himself, and certainly England's most renown healer. His reputation is worldwide. You'd do well to read his book."

I took the book home and began to read. Up to this time, I really had no convincing evidence of how powerful Spirit Healing can be. Yes, Kath had been healed of her kidney condition, but self-suggestion or the placebo effect couldn't be ruled out. As for my son Karl's eyes, a child will believe everything a parent says; a case of mind over matter. Nothing dramatic or out of the ordinary happened in healing circles at South Elmsall or Normanton, either. Any 'minor miracles' could be explained away in the same rational terms as self-suggestion or placebo. And I had no evidence of being a conduit for God's healing power. I hadn't yet felt anything like energy or power passing through me. Even to this day, I have yet to feel anything but a state of relaxation.

But Harry Edwards was a different world — no, his was an entire universe. While I had some success with minor aches and pains, Harry Edwards' success with "incurable" conditions was astonishing. The case histories he described demonstrated that there is no limit to the power of Spiritual Healing. The same energy that cures a headache can just as easily be called upon to heal cancers, tuberculosis, AIDS, leprosy or any "incurable" disease. It would work as effectively on brain tumors as it would on stiff joints. There were no limitations, if we just allow it through.

Harry Edwards provided explanations of how Spirit Healing works, how it could be developed and why some healings failed. He discussed Spirit Healing in relation to the church and medical community, talked about its divine purpose and made distinctions between mental healing, faith healing and paranormal healing. His information answered all the questions that arose in my mind as I went through the chapters. It was a textbook on every possible aspect of Spiritual Healing, and it took weeks to even begin to understand the information. I read and reread it, and sent off for every book this great man had written. He set me on fire!

A BIG MIRACLE HAPPENS

A couple of days before the book was due to be returned to the church library, our local paper ran a feature story about a former beauty queen, Maralyn Mount, who was suffering from a rare form of cancer in the lower abdomen. She was not responding to hospital treatment and her doctors gave her only three months to live.

I looked at the picture of her husband, Steve, holding their two young children. My heart went out to the family. Suddenly, a breath of hope blew through me. If they only knew about Harry Edwards, it might save her. If I gave them this copy of *Spirit Healing* and it had the same impact that it did on me, I might be able to help them. I had a daring thought. The Mounts lived only a few miles away in Mapplewell. I would go to their home and present her with the book.

Despite my good intentions, the short drive was torturous. I became anxious and uncertain. Doubting voices began hissing negative chatter. What if they scorned *Spirit Healing*? Suppose they think I am sort of a nut! What if . . .? What if . . .? What if . . .? My nerves were on overload.

Several cassettes were scattered over the front seat of the car. If I was going to do this, I decided, I needed to calm down. My favorite cassette at that time was *Canadian Pacific*, an American Country & Western album by George Hamilton IV. I loaded it in the cassette player and punched the play button. The music had an immediate, calming effect as I drove through the village streets to the fog-shrouded highway.

Finding the house was easy, keeping my courage up wasn't. I sat in the car for over an hour while George Hamilton sang about love, wounded hearts, woods, rivers and mountains, and I struggled with my all-consuming fears.

"Hell with it!" I said as I silenced the music, strode up to the door and knocked. An ashen young man opened the door. I recognized him immediately as the man in the newspaper photograph. The article said he was a schoolteacher. He had the look of someone accustomed to being analytical and deliberate. My heart was banging in my chest, choking down the speech I had prepared while sitting in the car. I held up the book, and the words broke free.

"Mr. Mount, my name is Malcolm Smith. This book changed my life. I would like your wife to read this book." I pushed *Spirit Healing* toward him. "I think it will help her." His brow wrinkled and he pulled back slightly as I extended my arm.

"What the man in the book can do, I can do also," I blurted out.

Did I say that? Up to that moment, I had never thought once that I was in the same league as Harry Edwards. But the words shot up from some place deep inside me, stampeding through my nervousness with a force that wouldn't be denied. The look on Steve Mount's face remained unchanged, as if still trying to find a category to label this bizarre moment at his door.

Spurred by the adrenaline rush, words continued to race from my mouth, faster than I wanted. "If your wife thinks I can be helpful to her in any way, please telephone this number," I thrust a slip of paper with my phone number into his hand and hurried away.

When I arrived home, panic set in. Apart from my wife and kids and the sessions at the Spiritualist Church, all I had ever treated was an assortment of backaches and painful joints for some cousins and aunts. They had all gotten some relief, but what possessed me to tell this grief-stricken man that I can do what Harry Edwards did? The Mounts had enough distress without a longhaired stranger knocking on their door making exaggerated claims and offering false hopes. Overcome with guilt and bitterness toward myself, I sank into a deep depression and prayed that she would reject my offer.

One month to the day my telephone rang.

"Mr. Smith?" The voice was weak and tinged with desperation.

"Yes!"

"This is Maralyn Mount. Would it be possible to come and see you this afternoon?"

"Yes, of course." I answered instantly, but my heart sank. "Oh my God," I thought, "what have I done?"

We made an appointment for 2:30 that afternoon, and right on time a battered white car pulled up outside my house. I recognized the driver as Steven Mount. I felt physically sick as Maralyn Mount, supported by her husband, struggled up the garden walk.

Kath met them at the door and helped her to the settee. I cried inwardly when I saw her. This young woman was a pathetic, frail shell.

"Can you really help me, Mr. Smith?" Her eyes reflected her heartache and suffering. "Even if you can't I would settle for some peace of mind." Her voice was tired and weary. I thought she was going to die right there on the settee.

"I don't know if you can be helped, luv, but I will try."

Without compassion and the desire to help, there can be no healing. My heart went out to her, and a yearning to ease her suffering overtook my nervousness. A feeling of peace began to settle over me. "Remember what Harry Edwards showed you," I thought. "It's just as easy to do a big miracle as a small one, because it's the same Power for both." It was reassuring. But could I really deliver on my promise to Steve? Could I really do what Harry Edwards did?

Steve looked weary and grim. "Before you start with whatever you are going to do to her," he said bitterly, "I want you to know, as far as I'm concerned, Spiritual Healing is a load of rubbish, but my wife is dying and she knows it. Whatever she wants she can have."

Steve and I helped Maralyn up the stairs, and then we laid her on the bed. I placed my hands over the area of Maralyn's cancer and worked on her for about fifteen minutes while Steve watched with what appeared to be a faint hint of disgust on his face.

"How do you feel now," I asked as I took my hands away.

"I feel 'different,' the pain is less, but it's still there," she answered softly.

"The healing is progressive," I said. "Please keep in touch."

"I will. I promise."

I stood at the door and watched as they got into their little white car and drove away.

"That's the last I shall see of them," I said to myself. "The healing hadn't even moved her tummy ache."

That evening, the phone rang. It was Steve Mount.

"Could you come and see Maralyn this evening?"

He didn't say what was wrong and I didn't think to ask. I simply assumed that she had deteriorated. With no regard for the speed limit, I rushed to their home. With a heavy heart, I made my way up the path and knocked on the door.

"My God! What has happened?" I spluttered in amazement as the door opened. Maralyn Mount, bright-eyed and rosy-faced, smiled at me. She glowed with newfound health. Steve stepped from behind her and began apologizing for his disparaging remarks about Spiritual Healing. Maralyn was eager to share her story.

"After leaving your house, I started to feel very ill, like I had to vomit. I asked Steve to stop the car so I could throw up." I nodded my head. This was promising. Vomiting foreign matter is a dispersal sign which a healer has to look for when giving healing for cancer. "And when I got home, I was so hungry…."

"Nothing like this had ever occurred before throughout her illness," Steve interjected. He smiled and looked lovingly at Maralyn, then back to me. "We sat her down and she ate a three course meal. The kids and I were astounded. She hadn't eaten hardly anything for over two weeks."

I was awestruck — not just at what I was witnessing with Steve and Maralyn, but at the responsiveness of the Great Power demonstrated by Harry Edwards and described in his book! My God, I thought, what if I had driven away, what if I had never knocked on her door, she'd be dead now, and her family grief stricken. Indeed, there was a Higher Power, and it was unlimited — and responsive. I vowed I'd never turn back from this work, ever!

Maralyn read *Spirit Healing* during the four weeks she spent at the Royal Marsden, the world famous cancer hospital in Surrey. It is not possible to say that reading Harry Edwards alone cured her, but Maralyn will tell you that book gave her hope, strength, peace of mind and comfort through her darkest hours. There were many months of visits between the hospital and my home before she was pronounced clear of the aggressive cancer which almost ended her young life. Gradually Maralyn resumed her busy and happy life as a mother, and seven years after she was declared cancer free, she wrote a book about her illness and took on a part time job.

Maralyn taught me a lot, not only about healing, but also of courage and not giving in, no matter how big the odds. "I'm not bothered about dying, Malc," she once said to me. "I know I won't be going to Hell, I've already been there!"

If anyone reading this book is living in his or her private Hell, I say, "Fight your way out, no matter how unforgiving or impossible your condition seems. Beat the odds! You can do it, don't give in! Fight! Fight! Fight! Maralyn did, and so can you."

CHAPTER TWO

THE YEARS BEFORE

In England, most of the healers I know do their work voluntarily, in churches, or in the privacy of their own homes. Many provide house calls, traveling long distances in all weather, and neither ask for, nor expect a fee. Love and compassion is their motivation. Their rewards are not counted in monetary terms, but in a client restored to health, pain and suffering alleviated, and happiness brought to a household where only heartache and despair existed before. The rewards that most healers value are usually spiritual, rather than material. But what happens when a healer transfers from a full time, material employment to performing full time Spiritual Healing? Where does the money come from to pay the everyday bills? "Trust in the Lord!" "Trust in the Spirit!" are fine phrases. But it's not what your creditors want to hear when they are at your door demanding money you owe them.

What is the price of healing? More important, who pays that price? This is a question that would become mine to answer.

I came into this world on the 19th February 1946, by my reckoning, the product of V.E. Night celebrations. My Mum was thirty-six when she had me, her long-awaited child. Her happiness was complete - but it was not to last. Five days passed. Instead of regaining her strength, she was losing it. By the seventh day she began to have visions, or hallucinations. She told one aunt that Jesus had appeared to her and kissed her on the cheek, and went to my cot and placed His hand on me. By the tenth day she was so weak that it was obvious that her time was near. She asked, in a voice so weak and faint that Dad had to bend over her to hear it - to hold her baby. Dad placed me in her arms and she went to sleep, holding me - never to wake again.

I've been told that the vision my Mum had of Jesus standing by my crib shows from the start I was predestined to follow the healing path. But I say, the Christ is present at every birth, and every life and child is unique and special and comes in for a purpose. We are all blessed! I am not sure that who my mother saw was Jesus. I suspect rather it was the same being that Adele and the others have seen over my 24 years as a healer. I believe he is a high spiritual teacher who guides and directs my work from the Other Side.

My Grandmother Smith, a combination of Mother Theresa and Rocky Marciano, raised me. In spite of the tragic circumstances of my birth, my upbringing was a normal one for a lad born into straitened circumstances in a small Yorkshire mining village. Growing up with Grandma Smith was not easy for me — or her. I was stubborn, self-willed, liked to fight, and hated school. Grandma Smith spoiled me beyond belief. Whatever I asked for I got - and there was hell to pay if I didn't! I had a temper that could get red hot in seconds.

When I was around five years old, she asked me to go to the shop for some potatoes.

"Give me five pounds an' I'll go!" I shouted back.

"I'll give it to you when you come back," she countered, and put a slip of paper in my hand. It was a letter asking the clerk for credit.

I got the potatoes, but bringing them home was like dragging a dead elephant up the street. Only the thought of the five pounds spurred me on. As soon as I reached shouting distance of my Gran, I demanded my wage.

"When I get a treble at the track," she answered with a laugh. Gran loved playing the horses.

"Well get yer own bloody tatties!" I yelled back and threw the bag of spuds under a passing bus. My reward for that petulance was a good clobbering from Dad!

That was my life, a mixture of love and correction. I hated school, played truant more times than enough, only to get a crack on the head from Gran as she dragged me, yelling and screaming in protest, back to school.

My favorite pastime was fighting. I was pretty fat as a kid, and most "fatties" get picked on, but I was able to take on kids three and four years older and usually win. Sometimes those extra pounds count! I often strutted through the village with Pete, my bull terrier, looking for fights. We thought we were king of the hill.

When I was thirteen, my father caught me smoking. I got a strong talking to, so strong indeed that I have never smoked since. That same year I decided my goal in life was to become a millionaire and own a Rolls Royce. I knew I wanted a better life than a miner's wage could offer. I even wrote the stock exchange, asking for information on how to purchase stocks and bonds. They wrote back saying I was too young to invest in the market.

I left school at the age of fifteen. I wanted to work at the local coal mine in our village. Dad had other plans for me. He wanted me to have a trade and sent me off to work at a well-known engineering company in a nearby town. There I would start a 7-year apprenticeship as a mechanical engineer with a starting salary of $5.00 a week – less tax, union fees and other stoppages. On day one I was given the simple task of drilling holes in a metal sheet. Three weeks later I was still drilling holes in metal sheets. It was the most boring job I've ever had (excuse the pun). I hated it. I pleaded with Dad to get me a job at the village pit. Reluctantly he agreed, and I ended up working with him in the lamp room looking after and maintaining the miners' lamps.

When I turned eighteen, I trained as a miner and went to work on the coalface 3,000 feet below the surface. Imagine traveling each morning down a shaft the depth of two Empire State Buildings with room left over, and spending the rest of the day crouched down in a tunnel just 2.5 feet high. Coal mining was hard and dangerous, yet I derived a strange satisfaction at the end of each shift. Although I had achieved nothing visible from all those hours deep in the bowels of the earth, I knew that one mistake could injure or kill my mates, or me, and I had come out unharmed. I still treasure the memory of those days.

The unity and the humor of the men I worked with are beyond description. It was a very close-knit comradeship. The work was hard and the pay was good. On Saturday nights we would go on our regular spree at the pubs and strip joints. The first stop was always at the Great Bull in Westgate, then on to the Double Six, where brawls were as common as the full glasses. Then across the road we'd go to cheer on the strippers in the Dolphin, then finish off the night in the Crown and Anchor.

When I reached 21, I realized I was spending my money as fast as I earned it. If ever I was going to be a rich man and own a Rolls Royce, I needed to make a change. The Merchant Navy offered possibilities. When you are out at sea, I reasoned, you couldn't spend your earnings. I put in my application and finally found a berth on the mighty 'Queen Elizabeth.'

After nine months at sea with trips to New York and a cruise to the Caribbean, I married Kathleen Maxwell, my girl friend of three years. We were wed on March 28, 1968. Three weeks later I was on a cargo ship bound for a six-month's trip to New Zealand, then on to the States. We were well under way when we learned that it would be an eighteen-month voyage.

On arrival in Auckland an urgent telegram was waiting for me. It was from Kath, my new bride. Her brother Craig had been run over by an ice cream truck, dead at four years old. Kath was devastated.

My skipper said he could arrange a transfer to the 'Southend Star' leaving two days later for England. Unfortunately, it was moored at the other end of New Zealand and I hadn't the money for the airfare to get to there. Most of my wages were regularly transferred home.

I leaned over the ship's rail, wondering what to do, when a local docker, standing only a few feet away on the quayside, asked me why I was looking so glum. I poured out the whole story to him.

"Don't worry son, something'll turn up for you," he assured me and walked away.

I was still searching for a solution as I went back to my cabin. About a half hour later, there was a knock at the door. It was the docker.

"Here you are son, we've had a whip round for yer!" he said as he slapped a wad of money into my hand. "There's enough there to get yer to Bluff, an' a bit more. Buy yer wife a present from us all in Kiwi!"

I was speechless. My eyes fixed on the money in my hand, as I struggled to mumble a few words of thanks.

"It can't stay dark forever young 'un," he said and playfully tapped at my chin with his huge fist. "Our best for you and your wife." And then he was gone.

I never even knew his name, but I've thanked him a million times over for what he did for us.

When I got home, I put up my sea boots and "swallowed the anchor" as they say, and started looking for work. For a brief period I cleaned windows. And then, equally unsuccessfully, I worked as a route driver, selling bread, cream cakes and buns. This brilliant sales career ended one beautiful summer morning when a police car, with headlights flashing and a spinning blue light on its roof caught up to me and signaled for me to pull over. The officer ordered me out of the van and with an arm around my shoulder walked me to the rear of the truck. The back doors of the van were flapping open. Inside, not a tray could be seen. My entire load was strewn across the highway. He let me off with a warning, but followed me back to make sure I picked up every bit of my 'rubbish' as he termed it.

Most of my wage for that week went to pay for the damaged goods. The next week I lost my biro pen. When I asked for a replacement the foreman answered, "If you don't have a pen, you have a problem, lad." That was it.

"Well it's your problem now, pal." I growled back and shoved my day's receipts into his hand. "I quit!"

After that, I toyed with the idea of going back down the pit. After a long discussion with Kath, I rejoined the Merchant Navy and set sail on the *King Alexander*, a floating scrap yard of a vessel bound for Holland, then to the breakers yard. I learned from some of the crew that Shell Oil was looking for crewmembers to work on their tankers in the Far East. I had a successful interview at Shell House in London and in June of 1969, I was flown out to replace a sick crewmember on the oil tanker *MV Amoria*. She was loaded with napalm gas, jet fuel and petroleum destined for American bases in the inland waterways of Vietnam. Our first port of call was

Saigon, then we traveled up the war torn coast to Da Nang, Cameron Bay, and other U.S. occupied ports. Since it was a war zone, the wages were extremely good, but the ship was always a target for the Vietcong rockets. Our sister ship, the *Amastra*, had been sunk in a rocket attack without loss of life.

During the eight months at sea, I managed to save enough money to pay the deposit on a luxury bungalow. It sold for $6000, a colossal sum at that time — and it made my Dad crazy. With a beautiful home and a new wife, it was harder for me to return to sea, but I needed to pay off my massive mortgage.

I took a position as a pump man on an oil tanker. The hours were long, often thirty-six hours at a stretch, but the pay was good. My job was emptying tons of oil at our port of call. This kept me on the ship at port, instead of prowling the bars. If I was ever going to be a millionaire — or pay off the mortgage, it wasn't going to happen by blowing my paycheck with my mates.

In May 1972 our first child, Adele, was born - a beautiful girl. The comfort and love of my family made it harder and harder to go back on the tankers. By 1973, Kath was pregnant with our second child, Karl. I decided to hang up my sea boots again, and went back down the mine. At a miner's wage, we could not afford to stay in the bungalow, so I sold it for $3,000 more than I paid for it, and moved into a modest terraced house next to Dad, in Ryhill. Kath went back to her old job in the mills at Wakefield.

I wasn't too happy at the pit, so it seemed like good fortune when I met an old mate, Raymond Johnson, a brick mason. He had left his employer to strike out on his own. Ray was now a builder. I explained my situation to him, and over a cup of tea, we decided to go into partnership. For our first venture, we bought five rental units on the same row as my father lived. They were cheap. I invested the profit from selling the bungalow, but I was still a few hundred pounds short of my share. I borrowed half from a small loan company with an interest rate at twice the bank's, and Dad lent me the rest.

I couldn't give up my job in the pit, so the work of renovating the houses was done in our spare time. Raymond promised to supply the labor to modernize the houses, but after he put up the additions at the rear of them, I saw little of him. My father and I labored three long years on the project until he died on October 1st, 1978. His dog, a big German Shepherd Labrador mix, knocked him into a table, and he broke three ribs. This went into pneumonia and heart failure.

My Dad was a tough, silent kind of man and not into metaphysics at all. The night before he died, he had an out-of-body experience. The experience frightened him. We lived close to each other, only a house between us, which my Dad owned. When I saw him that morning, he looked as if he had taken a turn for the worse. He was on the couch. He hadn't even pulled out his fold out bed.

"Dad, are you all right?"

"I've been up on the ceiling," he said, "looking down on myself."

"Dad, I'm going to call for an ambulance."

He shook his head, as if he knew he was losing his grip on life, on staying alive.

"Where have I been?" he asked. He was disoriented. "It was so dark. I couldn't get back." He knew he had been somewhere outside his body, but I was too emotional to ask more about it. "Put your arms around me, son," he said faintly. I wasn't sure I understood him. I leaned closer.

"What did you say, Dad. I didn't hear you."

"I want you to put your arms around me."

I put my arms around him and held him with my face against his. A couple of minutes passed, and then I felt him leave. I started immediately to give him "mouth to mouth" resuscitation for about five minutes, and then his eyes fluttered. I had brought him back.

I called a neighbor to stand watch while I ran to a phone to call a doctor. When I came back, Dad was gone, and I could not revive him. I once was asked if, as a spiritual healer, I have ever brought anyone back from the dead. I said yes, I brought my father back for ten minutes. This wasn't acceptable to the person who asked because of the short time he survived, but for me it is very real, even if it was just for a few minutes.

The death certificate said the cause of death was a stroke and pneumonia - it should have said simply that he died of hard work. Over the years, through several mediums, Dad has given me undeniable proof that he lives on in the Realms of Spirit. He was the greatest.

After my Dad passed over, I left the mines, and went full time into the construction business with Raymond. At last I had found my true calling, the building trade. Everything was going very well. Business was booming and the money was good. After three years, I fulfilled my childhood dream and purchased a second-hand Silver Shadow Rolls Royce. For me, the Rolls was a bulletproof insurance against failure. Anyone who owned a "Roller" was guaranteed automatic and lasting success. I believed it with the blind faith of a child. You never saw a poor man in a Rolls Royce, only the rich and successful. And now I had one.

Then, in February 1979, I had the fateful meeting with the psychic who told me I had healing hands. And everything began to change.

CHAPTER THREE

THE FORMS OF HEALING

Spiritual Healing takes many forms. Contact healing, where the healer places hands on a client, is familiar to most people. There are many examples of it in the New Testament. Absent or distant healing is when the healer asks for the power to be sent to a person who is not physically present. When we pray for others we are performing absent healing. A third method is extremely controversial. This is known as trance healing, or psychic surgery, and is widely practiced in the Philippines and Brazil. In trance healing, a spirit doctor, or guide, takes over the body of the healer. The healer acts as a medium, or physical channel, enabling the spirit doctors to perform 'operations' on a physical, mental or emotional condition of the person seeking help. It is bloodless, painless, and offers a complete effect and success in many cases. In recent years, the medium George Chapman, with his spirit control Dr. Lang, has been the most well known in England.

Right from the beginning, I had adequate proof that the healing energy could be directed by thought over a distance. Early in 1980, a friend of a friend in a neighboring village, Mrs. Mary Bloomfield, asked if I would send out absent healing to her mother. Her mother, then aged 69, had suffered for years with such bad circulation that gangrene had developed in two toes on her right foot. Her doctors recommended surgery to amputate the toes. Due to her mother's age and general condition, Mary, quite naturally, was very worried. She requested my help, and I agreed.

Each night at 10 p.m. I sat and asked for healing to be given to Mrs. Annie Dawson who had gangrene in her toes. I wasn't experienced enough with absent healing to know that, providing the healing thought requests are sincere, just a couple of seconds will suffice. For six nights I sat at the same time for some twenty minutes asking for dispersal of the gangrene on Anne Dawson's toes. Some nights I felt overshadowed by a comforting presence. It is a feeling I have enjoyed many times since. Around 7 p.m. on the seventh night, the telephone rang. It was Mary Bloomfield. She was very excited. The family doctor had just come to the house to examine her mother's toes, and not a trace of the gangrene was present.

"The gangrene's gone. Malc, it's a miracle! When her doctor removed the bandages from her foot, he said, 'This is a miracle.' Those were his own words, Malc. A miracle!"

The gangrene left her body and never returned. It was a complete healing.

Mary finally told her mother that she had received absent healing.

"Yes! I know!" she answered.

"But how did you know?"

"Every night, just after 10 p.m.," Anne replied, "I could feel a warmth and comfort around my foot. I knew it wasn't coming from me. It wasn't from a human source."

HELPFUL BEINGS

Sometimes the Presence takes on an individualized form. I was asked to visit the wife of a surgeon. She was dying from an incurable disease of the nervous system. I traveled down to her house at Bromley in Kent. She was suffering greatly and very weak. I gave her healing for 30 minutes, keeping my hands a few inches from her body. When the session was over, I left immediately for Yorkshire because of a business commitment.

That night she woke up in agony with tremendous pains in her hands.

"Good God, help me!" she cried out. Suddenly, her room became bathed in a comforting light, and two beings appeared and walked up to the side of her bed. They took hold of her hands and gently began to manipulate her fingers. A third man, whom she described as being 'tall and with a beard,' stood a few feet away watching. Within a few minutes her pain vanished and she fell asleep again. A few hours later the pain was back in all its ferocity - but so were the 'doctors'. They repeated the massage on her fingers, the pain gradually eased and she had her best night's sleep in years.

When I spoke to her several months later, she was still very much alive, and working part time.

"What does your husband think of this?" I asked.

"He won't speak of it," she answered. "But I'll tell the whole world if need be."

I have complete and utter faith in absent healing. I once received a telephone call from a woman in Mirfield, Yorkshire who was obviously in great distress. She had discovered her ninety-four-year-old father lying unconscious on his kitchen floor suffering a massive internal hemorrhage. She rushed him to the hospital where the doctors pronounced him too far gone to be helped. They gave him an hour to live at the most and suggested that she sit with him till he passed.

She had seen me on television some weeks before and had made a note of my telephone number. She made a desperate call and pleaded for absent healing. I responded immediately and within thirty minutes, her father's hemorrhage stopped. Four days later he signed himself out of the hospital.

Sometimes I become involved in circumstances entirely beyond my control, and of which I am completely ignorant.

One Sunday afternoon, an elderly lady was brought to my house by her daughter. I judged her to be in her early seventies, and she could barely manage to hobble on her two lightweight crutches. Her daughter explained that her mother was crippled with arthritis. I spent some twenty minutes directing energy to her by placing my hands over the major energy centers of her body, the head, heart, solar plexus and up and along the spine. Once her pain had left, I asked her to stand up and walk.

"Pass me my sticks then, please."

"You don't need them," I said.

From the look on her face, I could tell she thought I was a lunatic. Eventually, with her daughter's urging, she took a few steps without her crutches, and walked into my kitchen and back to the front room quite normally and without any pain. The two had a little weep as they were leaving. I promised to call and see her a few days later. Then I had to chase after the car with her crutches in hand. She had left them behind!

Four days later I called at her council flat only a mile or two from my house. I knocked on the door and it was opened by the old lady crouching and supported on her crutches. My heart sank. The healing hadn't held.

She stuck her head out into the corridor, and looked both left and right.

"Come in quick, lad!" She grabbed me by the arm and pulled me inside.

Once in the safety of her flat, she threw down the crutches on to the settee and walked across the room without any signs of discomfort.

"How are you feeling?" I asked.

"Haven't felt better for years, son!"

She saw I was puzzled, and explained that she was receiving a weekly disability pension.

"If word gets about that I'm healed, they'll take it off me," she said. "I got to pretend I need my 'sticks.'"

I promised not to tell a soul, making myself an accessory after the fact. Two years later she still did not need crutches, although she used them constantly to give herself financial support.

About this same time, another woman with a walking problem and a state pension asked me for healing. Flo (not her real name) had broken her leg. It had been set, but did not knit, causing her leg to be crooked. She refused to let the physicians break her leg again and reset it, so they provided her with a steel caliper to give her some support.

I visited her one Saturday afternoon. I followed her into the house and watched as she led me into her living room. She looked awkward and in pain. I sat her down and asked her to roll up her slacks so that I could see the extent of the damage. Her leg was very badly twisted, and the iron brace prevented me from placing my hands on her leg. When I asked her to remove the caliper, she refused. She was afraid I would hurt her. I tried to persuade her to remove the iron to no avail.

"The only alternative then is absent healing," I explained. "It's quite likely that your leg might feel very warm at night time. On the other hand, you might not feel anything at all."

A few days later she was watching television with her husband. Her leg began to get warm, and then it grew hot followed by a noise like creaking bones. Even her husband heard it.

"It's that lad wi' his absent healing," she shouted at her now bewildered husband. "Phone 'im up and tell 'im to stop it. I don't want it, it's frightening me!"

I had written my telephone number on a slip of paper for her, but try as he may, he could not find it anywhere, not that it would have mattered. It was out of my hands. The heat and the creaking noises continued unabated for almost 20 minutes. When it was over, Flo rolled her trouser leg up way above the caliper. Her crooked leg was now straight.

"Malc, I wanted to shout it from the roof tops." She smiled broadly and brightly. "I wanted the world to know, I'm healed! I'm healed!" She paused, and her face took on a more sober look. "But then, I realized I could lose my state pension if people got to know about it."

Flo discarded her caliper and has never needed it since. As for claiming the state pension she is not really entitled to, well I suppose that is her problem. There was a miners' strike going at the time, and lots of people were out of work. No doubt, she needed the extra cash. Who am I to judge her motives? I'll give her full credit though, when the story of my healing broke in our local paper, she told the reporter over the telephone every detail except her name and address - for obvious reasons.

When people enjoy a secondary gain from being ill, — a pension, attention, or control over others because of their condition — they will reject the healing energy. The benefit they derive from their illness is more important than returning to health. This is one of the reasons why some healings fail. However, Flo and the elderly lady managed to keep both.

There are differing types of fear about Spiritual Healing. Fear of the unknown I can understand, but when a person is afraid to tell their loved ones that they have been treated in a spiritual and unorthodox manner, it leaves me frustrated and perplexed.

One winter evening, I went to see a young woman suffering from Hodgkin's disease - cancer of the lymph glands. Normally this type of cancer responds well to orthodox medical treatment, usually within a few months. She had been having treatment for over two years with no positive results. The concern grew larger that she might not respond to whatever her physicians had to offer.

With little hope being offered at the hospital, she came to my house three times over a six-week period before she was due back for tests at the hospital, as she had done periodically over the past two years. Imagine everyone's surprise when her tests revealed no trace of the terrible disease. Month after month she returned to the hospital for tests, each time she was told the same news - "There is no sign of the illness!"

A reporter from our local paper asked me if he could talk to someone who had received healing for a serious illness. My thoughts immediately went to her.

Her life had been saved, I reasoned. Of course she'll want to share her story. It will give hope to others who may be suffering in a similar way. I phoned her with the request, and, to my surprise, she refused.

"My husband is against Spiritual Healing or anything like it. He would be upset if he knew I had been to see you."

I couldn't believe it. Why wouldn't he be overjoyed to know what spared his wife's life? Why couldn't she find the courage to share her story? Who knows what help or inspiration she may have given other souls suffering with hopeless situations.

On the other hand, I became a 'drug', an opiate to one man. Mr. Gordon Beecher was a fifty-two-year-old miner who had more or less recovered from a small operation to remove a cyst from his bladder. He was glancing through a 'Home Doctor' book, and turned to a chapter that dealt with the symptoms he had suffered. Soon he was convinced that he had cancer; it put his whole nervous system into a state of shock. Although Gordon had recovered sufficiently enough to return to work, he lost interest in everything and everyone. He stopped going out socially and no longer spent any time in his garden, which had always been a source of pride for him. All he wanted to do was to sit in his armchair, convinced that he had a serious complaint.

Weeks passed and Gordon's condition worsened. He would not eat. He slept no more than two hours a night. Even his good friend, a professional comedian, couldn't talk him out of it. In sheer desperation, his wife Iris telephoned me to see if I could give him healing that night. I was taking my wife out for a meal that evening and would be passing her house. I said I would drop by on our way out.

Gordon was sitting on the settee fully dressed as I walked in. Gordon and I knew each other, so I walked round to the back of the settee to place my hands on his head, assuming Iris already told him why I had come. She had not. Before he could even ask me what I was doing, he keeled over on the settee in a deep sleep. At first, I was concerned. I thought he had died. Iris just stared in awe.

He slept very well that night and I promised to call again the following evening. It seemed that the only thing that would put him to sleep were my hands placed on his head. Night after night when Gordon's bedtime came, I would go round to find him already in his pajamas. After a couple of minutes healing he would fall back on to his pillow, fast asleep. Considerable time passed before I could break him of these nightly visits. Finally Iris and I were able to convince him that he did not have cancer and that he was perfectly well. His interest in gardening returned, as did his social life and health, but for a short period I was both his sleeping tablets and an energy pill rolled into one.

People suffering from brain damage or brain tumors can also benefit from contact and absent healing. Graham Olgathorpe was a young man of thirty-two years of age when I first met him. From the age of ten he had suffered with an untreatable, slow growing brain tumor. His sister, Joyce Kirkby, telephoned me from their home at Wath, near Barnsley, to ask if I would help her brother. She told me of the constant pain he suffered, and that he had now gone deaf and blind. I offered to see him if she would provide the transport. Two days later Joyce turned up to take me to see her beloved brother.

I was shown into the little bungalow where Graham lived with his aged, widowed mother. Graham was sitting, lifeless it appeared, in an armchair. I placed my hands a few inches away from his head.

"Take your hands away from my head," he yelled in a loud, painful scream.

I looked at Joyce. "How does he know I have my hands above his head?"

She only shook her head as puzzled as I was. I spent about half an hour with him. By the time I left, the pain he had suffered for years was gone.

I arranged to see him again in two weeks. I had a holiday booked - but during that time Graham had deteriorated and slipped into a coma. I didn't know if I could help him once again, but agreed to try. This time I had Graham laid out on the settee. Very carefully I placed my hands on his head. Ten minutes passed.

Suddenly he opened his eyes. "Will you please take your hands away from me!" he said calmly. "And I would like a cup of tea!"

Joyce and his mother stared in amazement. This was the first time he had spoken in almost two weeks.

Three weeks later I had another urgent call from Joyce. The fluid in which the brain floats was leaking through his nose. The doctor had been sent for, and his examination indicated that once the fluid drained away, death would be imminent. I rushed to the house and placed my hands on his head. Within half an hour the clear fluid stopped dripping. Once again the medic had been proved wrong. Graham went on to live a lot longer than the doctors had predicted.

When his time came to pass into the world of spirit, it was pain free and dignified. His family attributed it to Spiritual Healing. The physical pain and torment had been lifted from him. For that alone I say, Thank God! I am certain that some people like Graham are placed on Earth and take on certain conditions in order to teach people lessons in patience, compassion, empathy, love and other spiritual qualities. I believe these people are among our highest spiritual healers and teachers.

The power of absent healing is as potent and as immediate as contact healing. While I was at Normanton Spiritualist Church, a lady asked me for absent healing for her father. He was suffering from cancer that was too far advanced to be operable. He was not expected to live more than another seven days. More from desperation than faith, she approached me for help. After hearing her describe the advanced stage of his cancer, I held little hope of bringing him any comfort, much less a cure. Still I promised to try, and at 10 p.m. that night I sat down and asked that healing could be directed to him.

The following day, Sunday, the lady went to visit her father. On entering the ward the Ward Sister asked her to come into her office to have a quiet word with her. She immediately panicked. Had her father died?

"Mrs. Rose," the sister said, "It's about your father. We do not know what happened - but during the night a great change has come over him for the better. Instead of only a week to live he could have twelve months!" Seven years later he was still alive and well.

This major episode taught me two things. First, that no matter how far gone a person is, if it is on the cards for that person to be healed, they will be; and second, perhaps the most important, for this change to take place in the man's condition so quickly, it proved to me that there is indeed a loving God who listens to our prayers.

You may think it strange, even after witnessing all those earlier "miracles," that it took this long to convince myself that the healings came through a divine source. Prior to becoming a healer, I was a person who shied away from any church and the religion that went with it. Even as I was witnessing the healing of my wife and children, even when Maralyn Mount and Mrs. Dawson were cured of their illnesses, there was doubt in my mind. Was it coincidence? Or mind-over-matter, self-suggestion or the placebo effect? In the cases of instant healing, my doubts were swept away.

Even today I am not what you would call a religious man, but from that day on I have never doubted that there is indeed a loving God who gives perpetual proof of His existence.

Earlier I described my daughter Adele's experience with a tall, bearded man who gave her healing and apparently watches over my clients. Many times he has appeared with cases involving absent healing. One of these incidents involved Mrs. Karen Dodd who requested absent healing for her twelve-month-old baby, Lee. Lee was suffering with asthma and a heart murmur. The baby had received regular checkups at the hospital but no treatment. Instead, the physicians suggested that when Lee was a few years older a small operation on his heart would probably correct his problem. That night I asked for the baby to be allowed to receive healing. At 10:30 p.m. Lee became restless. Karen heard him whimpering and went into her son's room to find a tall, bearded man standing over his cot with his hands on the baby's chest. She screamed and rushed back into her room to rouse her husband. When they got back to the baby, the night visitor had vanished.

Early next morning, Karen called on the phone, asking me not to send healing out; it had frightened them so much. The following week, his parents took Lee to the hospital for another checkup. The examination revealed absolutely nothing wrong with him. There were no asthma or heart problems. Several more visits produced the same report. Lee is now a normal, healthy lad. When I had the chance to ask Karen about the bearded man in Lee's bedroom, she told me it wasn't fear but the shock of seeing someone with her baby that had upset her.

"Looking back now, I regret that I telephoned you so hastily to cancel the healing," she confessed. Yet it is quite obvious from Lee's speedy recovery that the healing had continued.

HEALING CLOTHS

During my first two or three years of healing, the nonphysical aspect of absent healing bothered me for some considerable time. Most often the request would be made through a phone call from a loved one, and the healing energy would be sent out as promised, but the recipient frequently had no knowledge of what had occurred and was often kept in complete ignorance of the healing. There was nothing tangible in the process, nothing one could feel, or touch, it was utterly impersonal. What could be done to bring the recipient more into the process and make it real for them?

My cousin Jim was in his mid-sixties and suffered with arthritis in his knees. I'd visit him often to administer the energy, but couldn't always be with him as often as I felt he needed. I began hearing a voice in my head that kept saying, "use a cloth." I'd hear it over and over again. Finally, it put me in mind of the story in the Bible of the lady with the hemorrhage. She couldn't get close enough to Jesus to speak to him, so she reached out to touch his robe and was healed. When she touched his robe, Jesus felt power going from him, and told the woman her faith had healed her. For the woman, touching the garment was the same as touching Christ. Her intention manifested an insurge of healing energy. I wondered if I used a piece of cloth could it evoke or materialize the same energy as in contact healing? If so I might be able to use something like a handkerchief to stand in place of me. I later read in one of Harry Edwards' publications that this is a very old tradition. It is also noted in the Book of Acts (vs. 11-12) how St. Paul sent out prayer cloths and people were healed of illness and evil spirits. The use of prayer cloths has continued through the centuries.

"Jimmy, I need you to take part in an experiment," I told my cousin. "I am not sure it will work. Put this handkerchief on your leg when you go to bed and ask God to send his healing powers through the cloth." I gave Jim the cloth and told him to place it where he felt the pain, and to keep it there when he rested.

"When I reach out to touch you, my intention is to heal; the focus for the energy is through my hand. The focus of the handkerchief is the same. There's the intention, and you need it for the extra energy."

When I saw Jimmy a few days later he said that when he used the handkerchief he could feel warmth and a lessening of the pain. That encouraged me, and I began to give out handkerchiefs as a part of my distant healing ministry.

A handkerchief is something everyone carries; it is not a 'gimmick' and not expensive. How does it 'work'? You don't 'work' it, I don't 'work' it. When a person accepts a handkerchief and uses it, they are 'reaching out' for healing, the same as the woman with the hemorrhage. I suggest to people that they use the handkerchiefs only when they are in a receptive state, such as at bedtime, recuperating from an illness or when they are in prayer or meditating. Some people hardly notice that they are wearing theirs. Others, like my cousin, find that they seem to generate heat, sometimes to an uncomfortable level. Some just receive a comforting warmth. Another interesting phenomena connected with the handkerchiefs is that, for several people, once they felt healed, the handkerchief disappeared. One lady kept hers in a glass container with a lid. She always put it there, and then one day it was gone. She didn't need it anymore.

CONTACT AND ABSENT HEALING COMBINED

As my healing ministry progressed, I soon discovered a combination of contact and absent healing could bring powerful results. Little Lisa Stainforth was born with serious physical handicaps. She could not focus her eyes, nor could she communicate with her parents. For the first two years of her life, she suffered between fifty and one hundred fits each day. The drugs that were prescribed for her had little effect.

"They simply make her drowsy and looking like a floppy rag doll," her mother said. An electroencephalogram revealed an obstruction in the brain. Her eyes were examined with no result.

Lisa's parents approached me and asked me to give her healing. I immediately added her name to my prayer book, prayed for her nightly at 10 p.m., and administered hands-on healing. After three weeks, the fits stopped and never returned. Lisa began to sit more upright, hold her head up, and her sense of balance improved.

In addition to my treatment, Mrs. Stainforth took Lisa to a physiotherapist in Somerset for visual tests. The tests confirmed that her sight had improved. A second EEG examination showed the obstruction in the brain had cleared. The doctor was so surprised he checked to make sure he had not been given the wrong report.

Lisa continued to improve. She became aware of her surroundings and her vision improved to the extent that she was able to distinguish colors. Previously, she could only occasionally distinguish light from dark. Her limb movements became stronger and she began to speak. At the age of four and a half, Lisa was participating in a playgroup for the handicapped, swimming, painting and playing with other children. Spiritual Healing can be virtually instant, though sometimes the cure takes a long time - but what heartening improvements can be seen along the way!

Makala Midgley's condition was considered "incurable." Makala began to experience terrible pains in her legs at the age of two. Her parents were told that a nerve had wrapped itself around her spine. Seven years of hospital visits, x-rays, blood tests and a battery of drugs brought no relief. Her pain was constant and unrelieved. Her doctors finally told the unfortunate parents there was nothing more that could be done for their little girl. She would have to live with her condition.

When Makala's parents came to see me, they had never known a good night's sleep. Makala was a shy but bonnie looking child. I placed my hands on her head and commenced her healing. After ten minutes she appeared more relaxed.

"Are you in pain now?" Makala responded with a slow shake of the head, indicating she was not.

I produced a healing handkerchief and gave it to the Midgleys.

"Pin it to her nighty at bedtime. The handkerchief is a focus for the healing energy. Keep it on her body when she's resting or in pain."

Two weeks later I saw Makala again.

"Makala's pain is getting worse," Mrs. Midgley reported. "Every night the handkerchief becomes very hot, and perspiration just pours from Makala."

For the next two months, conditions remained the same. Makala gained relief while I treated her and between visits the pain returned. Finally, she slept through the night pain free for the first time in her young life. From that point on, the pain stayed away and her parents soon discovered they could discontinue the pain killing drugs that were prescribed for her. She no longer needed them. Her father called to make an appointment with her doctor to tell him he had not been giving Makala her prescriptions. Naturally, he was very apprehensive at what the doctor's reaction would be.

"Then how is she coping with her pain?" the doctor questioned.

"I've been taking her to a healer," he confessed, bracing himself for an angry outburst, and received an unexpected response. Enthused and with great interest, the doctor asked for more details!

On my next visit, Makala told me shyly that two or three weeks before, she woke up early in the morning to find 'a lady' standing at the side of her bed. She described the color of her hair and how she was dressed.

"How could you see all this when it was still dark in the bedroom?" I asked quietly.

"It was easy," she replied, "she was shining like light. She never talked to me or nothing, she just smiled at me and I smiled back. I closed my eyes and when I opened them again she was gone."

I wondered, was it her guardian angel?

CHAPTER FOUR

CAUGHT IN THE WHIRLWIND

By the end of 1981, my reputation as a healer had spread to many of the neighboring villages, and even beyond. Soon, it was impossible to respond to all those who required home visits. So I opened up my small row house as a healing clinic.

I made no charge. I didn't even ask for a donation, nor did I set hours. People showed up any time, day and night, no appointment necessary. For a few weeks the burden of traveling was lifted.

Meanwhile, Raymond and I had managed to buy a piece of building land in the village, enough to build ten new houses. But we had to get the plans passed and planning permission. Now I was working full time in the building trade with my partner. We got the go ahead to start the new project. The houses sold well and everything was going to plan; it seemed that our ship had finally come in.

When I finished my daily stint on the building site, I rushed home, took my bath, had my tea, and waited for the sick to visit me. I soon became aware that none of the many people for whom, week in, week out, sometimes for months, I had been making house calls ever came to my house. It was a great disappointment to me, but before long I knew I had taken on much more than I could cope with.

People were filling all three of my downstairs rooms, lining up along the path that led to my door. They arrived at all hours. When I got home from work, bush tired and looking like something the cat had dragged in from the alley, they were sitting in my house waiting for me. At first the idea of making my home a healing sanctuary felt like a good one, but within a few months it was apparent something had to be done. There were just too many people coming for healing.

Meanwhile, I quickly learned that a Rolls Royce tends to bring out the darker side of a person's character, especially in a working class neighborhood like mine. I often got a two-finger salute and abuse hurled at me from other motorists and pedestrians. Even my wife refused to travel in it. "How on earth can you own a Rolls Royce and live in a row house?" she asked more than once.

I traveled a lot to people's homes to give healing, and occasionally drove the Rolls to them. The visits were always free of charge, but the people I treated didn't realize this until after the healing. Sometimes I thought I could feel their resentment. One lady, Isobel Donaldson from Brierley, telephoned to ask for healing. When I pulled up to her house in my metallic Rolls, she asked in her soft Scottish burr,

"Is that your car, son?"

"It is, luv." I proudly replied.

"Och! Then I'm not sure I can afford your services, Mr. Smith."

"It won't cost you a penny," I answered.

Her initial antipathy quickly vanished, and soon she was cured of a painful spinal condition she had suffered from for years. Her husband Bill owned Britain's top champion show car, an immaculate MGB GT V8. They invited Kath and I for dinner, and they remained two of our closest friends.

THE DYING NURSE

Small cracks in my family life began to appear. Even though I was made aware of them, I was blindly prepared to sacrifice everything to continue with what I felt I was put on earth for - healing the sick. Looking back now I realize how utterly selfish and unreasonable I was toward my wife and children. They had no privacy - nor did the people coming for healing. The TV was not allowed on for fear of distracting the healing, the children often were made to go to bed early, so that they would not annoy the people waiting for healing. While other families were out on lovely summer evening walks or on weekend picnics, my wife was brewing tea, or making coffee for the people who were coming far and wide for healing. Whenever a rare opportunity occurred to take Kath and the children somewhere nice, I refused. All I wanted was to go to work, come home and heal the sick in the evening. Nothing else mattered. When I wasn't healing, I was reading books about it. All the things in life that I had enjoyed before no longer mattered. I was a raging current of emotion. I knew that stress was taking its toll on the family and I was becoming bad tempered and antisocial at home and at work.

Ultimately I became a casualty of my own obsession. I became ill with bronchitis and nervous exhaustion. The down time brought on by my illness gave me space to face myself. I began looking at what I was doing and what changes were needed. It was my darkest of dark nights. And then, a change of direction occurred, and the sun was up and shining again.

A few days after I had shaken off my illness, Mr. Dennis Thompson, a gentleman in his early forties, telephoned me one evening. His wife, Mary, was dying from liver failure and had only a few weeks to live. Mary had been a nurse at Fieldhead Hospital. One night, while on duty in one of the wards, she pulled a muscle in her back while helping to lift a patient into bed. She was given a drug for the severe pain — and suffered an almost fatal reaction. Three specialists confirmed that her liver was virtually rotting away, an effect of the drug.

No operation was possible. Nor could Mary be given any other drugs to combat the original back pain, the liver pain, or relieve the distressing side effects. The risk was too great. She was dying and suffering excruciating, unrelenting pain. The doctors recommended Mary be admitted to a hospice facility. Dennis was a qualified male nurse. He and his three children, twenty-two-year-old Karen, fifteen-year-old Donna, and six-year-old Tracy, an adopted daughter, decided to bring Mary home to die, surrounded by those she loved.

"Mary's weight has dropped from 136 pounds to 84 pounds," Dennis said with deep concern. "She's become so frail she can hardly bear the weight of two blankets and lacks the strength to feed herself."

It was obvious he had been under a great strain for some time. "To be honest," he continued, "I can't see how this healing could possibly do any good, but I promised the kids I would do whatever I could to save her. Will you see her?"

"Yes," I said. His anguish and despair were palpable.

"When?"

"Right now, if that's all right."

The Thompsons lived just a couple of miles down the road. I grabbed my coat off the hook and headed for their house through the dense evening fog.

Dennis greeted me somberly at the front door and took me to the stairs. "Look, she doesn't even know you are coming," Dennis said, stopping midway up the stairs. "I'm not even sure she's ever heard of you, does it matter?"

Even if it had mattered, it was too late to do anything about it now. I followed him into the bedroom.

"Mary, this is Malc Smith, he's a faith healer!" Somehow he struggled out the halting introductions. Mary's skin was a yellow pallor, her eyes sunk deep into the sockets, and tears of pain slid down the hollows of her cheeks. She tried to raise her hand, but the effort was too much.

"Sorry … I … I've got … an … awful headache," she whispered hoarsely. Her voice became a choking sob. "Who will look after my kids? I don't want them put in a home!"

I put my hands gently on her forehead. "Listen Mary, if I thought I couldn't help you, I wouldn't be here."

"Why are your hands so hot, Mr. Smith?"

Before I could explain, she turned to Dennis. "My headache!" Her voice was trembling with excitement. "It's gone!"

I felt an instant wave of gratitude, and a new flush of confidence. My hands were still on her forehead.

"Mary, now where do you feel the most pain?" I asked.

She indicated the base of her spine and across the stomach and grimaced. "You'll not be able to do much for that. I've had this pain every hour of every day for months."

I placed one hand at the base of her spine and the other on her stomach. She lay shaped in a deformed fetal position.

"Her spine's locked in that shape," Denni
without my help. She hasn't been able to walk

In a few seconds the healing energies begar
hands. This time it was not the great heat she had
intense coldness. Obviously a different form of h
needed for this problem. It was so cold, she said, th
her, especially at the base of her spine, and in her   ...ne
effect was immediate. For the first time in weeks Mar) ...s without
pain. The tears flowed again. They were tears of joy.

"Mary," I said reassuringly, "It may be true that you lost a few
battles along the way, but we haven't lost the war."

I stayed with Mary a little longer. We talked, mostly about
Spiritual Healing, until my watch showed me it was midnight. The
doctors had told Dennis Mary wouldn't live to see Christmas. With
this 'death sentence' hanging over her, I agreed to visit her every
night until she was cured - or passed into spirit. Hours later, she was
still experiencing the coldness. She would feel it many more times
over the next few weeks.

As promised, I returned the following night. Mary appeared a
little brighter. She had slept and eaten better than she had for quite
a while. Her pain had returned, but not as severely! This is a pattern
in my healing process. The effects of the first session soon wear off.
With the second session, the results tend to stay longer. Each session
helps move the healing process further along. By the fourth session,
an individual will either receive 100% of what they came for, or
see some measure of progress, small or great, and make a choice
whether they want to continue or not. If nothing has happened by
the fourth session, it is unlikely that anything will occur on the fifth
or sixth. Spiritual Healing is not for everyone.

On my fourth visit, Dennis took me aside.

"Do you know anyone who might be interested in buying my
car?" he asked quietly. "If I can sell the car we can have an early
Christmas as a family for the last time. I could make it a Christmas
the kids and I will never forget."

Dennis had been off work so long looking after his dying wife
that their savings were exhausted. The only valuable thing left was

...nd he was ready to sacrifice it to give his wife and kids a Christmas treat - even if it was only mid-November.

"I'll make inquiries," I promised. Then we went upstairs to give healing to Mary. As I placed my hands on her head, a deep knowing possessed me.

"Mary, you are not going to die. You're going to make it through."

"But how can that be Malc?" she asked in a tiny, tired voice. "I have to be spoon-fed, I can't stand, or walk. I'm having blackouts!"

"I don't know how I know," I answered, "but in my heart there is not a shred of doubt you're going to be well." I thought I saw a flicker of hope flash in her eyes.

I gave Mary healing and left her with her daughter Tracy holding her hand. The little girl had sat with her Mum every spare hour of the day since Mary had been sent home to die.

Less than an hour after I left their home, little Tracy burst into the room where Dennis sat, reading the paper. She threw herself into his arms, uncontrollably crying in huge, heartbreaking sobs.

"It's my Mum!"

Fearing the worst, Dennis took hold of her shoulders. "What's wrong Tracy?"

Tracy started sobbing.

"What about her, what's happened?" Dennis asked, with a hint of panic.

"She - she's got out of bed on her own, Dad," she answered, brushing away her tears. "She can walk and her back is straight, it's not bent anymore!"

Dennis took the stairs two at a time with Tracy at his heels, and rushed into the bedroom, where Mary was standing on her feet.

"I'm going to make it, Dennis! I'm not going to die." Dennis fought back the tears as he watched his wife walk slowly towards him. "I'm going to get better, after all." Emotion choked back any reply. Dennis pulled his wife gently towards him, broke away momentarily to scoop Tracy into his arms, and together they hugged and kissed and wept. For Mary Thompson Christmas had, indeed, come early.

Many more weeks passed before Mary could go about her everyday duties. There were many fluctuations in her condition that at times gave rise to concern, but there was humor too.

One night their bed began to shake.

"What are you doing, making the bed vibrate like that?" asked Dennis.

"Shush! It's the spirit doctors," replied Mary, who accepted it as all part of the healing treatment.

"Don't talk crazy, woman!" Dennis jumped out of bed and switched on the bedroom light. To his amazement, even with the light on, the bed continued to move as though some unseen hand was rocking it.

"Told you it was the spirit doctors!" said Mary, completely unconcerned. "Now, switch off the light, and get back in bed!"

"You've got to be kidding! I'm not sleeping in a haunted bed!"

"Don't be daft, it's not haunted, it's part of the healing."

"Well, they aren't healing me!"

And Dennis, poor old lad who once told me that he was afraid of nothing, spent a long cold night sleeping on the settee downstairs.

Eventually Mary became well enough to return to her job as a nurse and pass her driving test. Although the healing saved Mary from an early grave, it did not give her a complete cure. To this day, her liver cannot cope with drugs; even mild ones like aspirin can make her quite ill. Any time she feels poorly, be it with flu or a backache, they give me a ring and I go along and give her healing.

"YOU ARE OUR LAST HOPE, MR. SMITH"

Throughout this same period of 1983 and 1984, several major healings stand out in my memory.

Mavis Heeley's son, Paul, had been very seriously injured in a road accident nine months previously. He was completely paralyzed from the neck downwards, was suffering from irreparable brain damage, and had been in a coma since the day of his accident. Mavis and her husband, Vincent, were told that nothing more could be done for him. In the unlikely event of any sort of recovery, his life would be spent as a "cabbage." For the whole nine months of his hospitalization, his mental condition was in limbo; he responded to nothing, to no one.

I listened carefully as his mother pleaded for help. "You are our last hope, Mr. Smith, there is nowhere else to go. Please, will you see him?"

I agreed to visit Paul at Pinderfields Hospital in Wakefield. At seven o'clock the next evening I stood with two heartbroken parents at the bedside of a young man. Twenty-one years old, tragically robbed of a future, his life was fast fading with each passing week.

I stood in silence for several minutes. Tubes and wires protruded from every part of his body. His eyes were wide open, fixed to some imaginary spot on the ceiling. His fingers were clasped so tightly into the palms of his hands that pieces of sponge rubber had been inserted to prevent his finger nails digging into his flesh. It looked hopeless. If, as some people claimed, Spiritual Healing was nothing more than self suggestion, his loving parents, his brothers and sisters, all his friends, would surely have been able to achieve something by now. Instead, Paul was deteriorating weekly.

I gave a deep sigh of despair, and moved forward to the side of his bed. I put my hands over his head and asked God to allow Paul to receive healing. I prayed that the guides be given the knowledge to overcome the paralysis and coma. The guides don't have healing energy of their own; they administer God's healing energy. They have to work with the acquired knowledge they may have gained while physically incarnate or through continued learning in the spirit realm. You can't have healing energy going into a body without intelligence to back it up. The guides need to know how to heal specific diseases, so they've got to acquire some knowledge from God to use that energy to overcome the problem. The closest example I know of is the radiation given in hospitals. It's a very crude form of healing energy, but behind it is intelligence: the radiologist needs to know how much radiation to use and for how long. The guides use God's energy in the same way. If it were direct intervention by God, we would have 100 percent healing every time. We don't. In most cases, the improvement ranges from slight all the way to 100 percent. You never know what you're going to get.

I kept my hands on Paul's head for a few minutes, and then moved them slowly down his spine to allow the healing energy to flow into him. Ten minutes passed. I leaned over and spoke into his ear.

"Paul, I want you to move your right leg for me, please."

Perhaps two minutes passed, and then his right leg, from the knee downward, moved slightly.

"That was a spasm," his mother said, yet the look on her face betrayed her hope.

"Paul, I would now like you to move your left leg for me."

Again, some moments passed. His left leg moved a few inches across the bed.

"Thank you, Paul, stretch your fingers for me."

Mavis looked up from her son. "I'm afraid even the nurses have problems trying to do that, Mr. Smith." Her voice was tight with emotion. "It usually takes two of them to do it." As she spoke, Paul slowly uncurled the fingers of his right hand.

"Mr. Heeley, please place your hand on Paul's open fingers." Vincent reached down and gently placed his hand over his son's. The energy in the room grew more intense.

"Paul, I have your Mum and Dad here with me. Turn your head and look slowly at them."

Slowly, very slowly, Paul turned his head toward his parents. Tears ran down their faces. For the first time in nine months, he understood and responded to words said to him — and moved limbs the doctors said were paralyzed!

"Now, Paul, squeeze your father's hand."

Ever so slowly, Paul's fingers moved inward. Mr. Heeley was overcome. He quietly disengaged his hand, walked over to a quiet corner of the ward and sobbed.

I arranged to visit Paul on a regular weekly basis. After each visit, a small but definite improvement was obvious for all to see, including the specialists who had treated him. They were at a loss for words. Just when we thought Paul was on the mend and out of danger, I received a telephone call from the hospital. It was Mrs. Heeley. Paul had been taken dangerously ill and was not expected to live through the night. His parents rushed to his bedside.

"Would you like a priest to administer the Last Rites?" the attending nurse asked.

"Not until we have spoken to Mr. Smith." Their reply left the nursing staff puzzled.

My heart was heavy as I listened to Mavis describe her son's grave condition. Then, quite suddenly, I 'saw' Paul sitting up in bed. I didn't realize it then, but the guides had projected the image into my consciousness. It's like someone on the mountaintop that can see far ahead sending directions to a person on the ground.

"Don't worry, Mavis. By the morning Paul will be O.K. And again the doctors will be mystified."

By the following morning, the danger had passed. It was as if nothing had happened to Paul to warrant the hospital sending for his parents. The doctor in charge admitted to Mrs. Heeley that her son had them all 'puzzled.'

Four years later, Paul was still hospitalized but he could navigate an electric wheel chair, feed himself and pick out words that were shown to him. His brain is making a slow but definite recovery.

TALL MAN WITH A BEARD

Early in 1983 I received a telephone call from Mr. Graham White. He had heard about me from a mutual friend, Bill Donaldson, who worked with him at the Prince of Wales colliery at Pontefract. He said his daughter 'Jacky' had developed cancer in her leg and chest, and that she was not responding to the treatments administered at their local hospital. Her condition was worsening.

The Whites lived on the outskirts of Manchester, about an hour's drive from my house. I had no car at the time, though this problem was easily overcome. Graham would fetch me.

Their home was very pleasant; its main feature was the living room with its beautiful stone fireplace and an elegant open staircase which curved round into the living room itself. Just a few feet away from the staircase, Jacqueline White, pale and weak, her eyes red and swollen with crying because of the pain, lay in her bed.

I knelt down beside her and placed my hands over the cancerous leg and then over her chest. A few minutes passed.

"Can you feel anything?" I asked.

"Yes," she said, "The pain is gone."

Graham and Pauline said nothing of the healing, but were obviously very grateful that their daughter's suffering was relieved. Jacqueline responded only when I asked her a direct question. It was a strange, quiet visit. As I prepared to leave, I took a handkerchief from my pocket, and put it in her hand.

"Jacky, this is a special handkerchief. When you use it, God will send you some healing energy. Just place it on you where you want the energy to go." I promised her I would be back next week, and started to leave. Pauline followed me to the door.

"Where do you reckon this healing comes from then?" Her voice was tinged with bitterness. I felt accused, as though I had done something wrong, something bad.

I shook my head slowly. "From God! There can be no other source."

"If there's a God, why has my child got cancer?" Her dread and bitterness burst forth. "If there's a God why has my child to suffer like this! Why has God walked out on us?"

I had no answer to relieve her misery and despair. Not then, anyway.

A couple of days before I was due to see Jacky again, I was reading 'Spiritual Healer,' a magazine with articles by Harry Edwards, testimonials and poetry, that comes from his healing sanctuary in Guildford. One of the pieces was 'Footprints in the Sand,' an inspirational story about a man's dream of walking with God on the seashore, and looking back and seeing many times there was only one pair of footprints in the sand. When he questions God about this, God replies those were the times He carried him through his difficulties. It is a famous story, and by now I think just about everybody in the world has heard some version of it. As I read the story, my stereo was playing a beautiful song called 'Peace.' The music and story blended together in a striking way, like an inspired composition. I knew I had my answer to Pauline White's unanswered questions.

It took me twenty hours of love and labor to dub the marvelous sentiments of 'Footprints' to the music of 'Peace.' I was determined to get it right, and indeed I did.

When I arrived on my next visit, the atmosphere was less tense and conversation became easier with the Grahams. Jacqueline was sleeping and eating better, and the pain in her leg had not returned. In fact, she had strength enough to sit up in bed and color some pictures in her books.

I gave healing to Jacky, and then handed Mrs. White my recording.

"What's this?" Pauline asked, looking puzzled.

"It's the answer to last week's question, why has God walked out on us?"

She put the tape into the recorder, and pushed the play button. Her eyes filled with tears as she listened, and then she broke down. "Yes!" she sobbed long before the tape was finished, "Yes, I understand now."

Jacqueline asked to listen. She thought it was the most beautiful story she had ever heard. The recording and the handkerchief became her two most treasured items. When I asked her why, she answered, "Because I get comfort from them both."

On my next visit, Jacky pointed to the stairway near her bed and told me she had a visitor.

"There's a man who comes and stands over there. He comes when everybody's gone to bed."

"What does he look like, Jacky?"

"He's tall, with a beard." Jacky described in exact detail the same being my daughter Adele and Mrs. Dodd and several others had seen.

"Does he speak to you?"

"No, he just stands there. I want to shout to my Mum and Dad but I'm afraid that he will come over to me if I do."

"How long have you been seeing him?" I asked.

"Since the first night you came to see me. I wanted to tell you about him before. I was afraid you would laugh at me and think I was silly."

I took her hand, "Don't be afraid, it could be Jesus, or a guardian angel sent to watch over you."

Although the figure never spoke, she continued to see him almost every night. All fear of him left her. Then one Friday night about ten o'clock, the telephone rang. It was Mrs. White.

"Malc, I've some bad news for you." Her voice was calm yet at the same time was charged with emotion. "Jacky passed away this afternoon."

I was stunned. I knew Jacky wasn't making the progress that I would have liked but there was some improvement over her original, steady deterioration.

"Jacky woke up quite excited," Pauline said, "and told me of the man on the stairs. Last night, for the first time, he spoke to her."

"He's great, Mum! He's ever so kind. He has promised to take me to a place that is ever so beautiful. He's coming for me at teatime Mum and I don't have to be ill anymore! Pack all my best clothes for me Mum, and will you iron my favorite dress please? I want to look nice when I get there."

"I didn't know what to think," Pauline said. "It was so strange, yet she was so happy and excited."

Pauline did everything her daughter asked. All through the day Jacky entertained herself with her coloring books. In the afternoon Jacky sat up in bed and helped her mother whisk up a cake mixture. Then, at about four-thirty Jacky asked to listen to the recording of 'Footprints.'

"He'll be here soon," she said, "and I'd like to hear Malc's record before I go." Pauline played her the tape. At about five o'clock Jacqueline became very excited.

"He's here Mum! He's come for me, I knew he would." Pauline turned and looked, confused. No one was to be seen.

"Mum I have to go now. Give me a kiss and give Daddy a kiss from me. Tell him not to cry."

Pauline leaned forward and kissed her daughter fondly. Jacky smiled at her mother, and lay back on her pillow.

"And that was the end, Malc. She died."

I struggled to hold back the emotion that was threatening to engulf me.

"I - I'm sorry the healing failed Pauline," were the only words I managed to say.

Pauline responded without hesitation. "Don't you ever say the healing failed, Malcolm Smith! Oh no Malc, the healing didn't fail. You took away my kiddy's pain and suffering. You took away her fear of death. You showed us also that there is no death. What happened today is the most beautiful and moving experience my husband and I have ever known!"

She asked me if she could keep the tape of 'Footprints.' The handkerchief I had given to Jacky was placed in her coffin.

"She would not want to part with it," Pauline said, "We will let her take it with her. Thank you for all you have done, Malcolm, and God bless you, always."

I bade her goodnight, replaced the telephone on its receiver, put my head down in my hands, and for the first time in seeing thousands of people, I broke down and cried.

CHAPTER FIVE

HAVERCROFT HALL

I lost count of the people who came to my home; in the final analysis it averaged about fifty per week. It was turning into a nightmare. I was working full time and trying to cope with all the people seeking healing seven days a week, and my family was suffering from the pressure. I didn't know how long this situation could hold together without a breakdown. Then Dennis Thompson came to the rescue.

Dennis called one evening to say that he had found an ideal place about a mile from my home to use as a healing center - Havercroft Parish Hall. For a small fee of $4.00 per hour, we could have the use of the main hall, kitchens and tearooms.

It's a dream come true, I thought. A huge weight lifted from my shoulders.

I decided to rent the hall on Sunday and Wednesday evenings. Sundays would be open to anyone and Wednesdays would be reserved for people suffering from serious or terminal illnesses. Because of the great volume of clients who appeared at my home I decided to enlist the help of other healers I had befriended in the earlier years of my ministry. Bill and Margaret Lloyd from Brierly Spiritualist Church were the most dedicated. They had been in Spiritualism most of their lives and were good, established healers in their own right.

The first Sunday over one hundred people attended. When a man who had been totally blind for seven years received his sight back after only a few minutes of healing, it was an emotional experience for everyone. Many in the room could feel the sweet presence of the Divine. For others, it was the first "miracle" they had ever witnessed. For them, it was like something out of the Bible. There was not a dry eye in the hall that afternoon.

Other healings were memorable, but not for the same reason. There was the lady who suffered from multiple sclerosis and had lost the ability to walk. Her husband ran a very successful newsagent's shop. Bill and Margaret Lloyd volunteered to make weekly visits to administer healing at her home. For ten months they unfailingly made their weekly pilgrimage in all kinds of weather until the lady was able to control her previously lifeless limbs and walk unaided. They neither asked for, nor were offered a single penny, not even for traveling expenses.

Bill asked if she would consider traveling over to our weekly healing services in Havercroft Parish Hall. He explained that while he and Margaret were traveling to see her every week, they could be giving healing to three or four needy sufferers. Reluctantly, she agreed.

On her first visit to Havercroft, she sat in my chair and I gave her healing. When I finished, she got up without a word of thanks and walked away. She stopped at the donation box on the table just outside the healing room, and took a pound note ($1.50 U.S.) from her purse.

"Could you change this for me, luv?" she asked Kath, my wife. "I want to put something in the donation box."

"I'm sorry," Kath said, "I don't have the change."

"What shall I do then?" she asked.

"That is entirely up to you, luv."

With that, the lady strode out of the hall with the pound note clutched in her hand. Apparently, ten months of personal visits and definite improvement in her condition were not considered worth a pound note.

The primary purpose of all Spiritual Healing is to arouse the soul, to stir the spiritual energies. Unless the root of the problem is addressed — and the root is almost always a spiritual or emotional imbalance — any healing can only be short-lived and superficial.

In Spiritual Healing, the energy goes first to the spirit and then is transferred back to the physical, but if the spirit isn't open and receptive, the healing will fail or only have a temporary effect.

As this lady strode out of the church, in a bit of a hurry to get away, I thought she must be very uncomfortable trying to convince herself that our services were not worth a pound note. All the mental effort will surely result in creating a block to continued spiritual flow.

Another unforgettable visitor to Havercroft was a lady, probably in her middle sixties, dripping with so much gold in the form of rings, bracelets and necklaces it was a wonder she didn't suffer from metal fatigue. She had been blind in her left eye for eight years. In the beginning at Havercroft, we were not allowed use of the side rooms, so our healing was carried out in public view on a small stage. I sat her down on my healing stool in front of some eight or ten people, and failed to restore her sight.

"That's the last I shall see of her," I mused as she marched off the stage, walked passed the donation tin without a sideways glance, and out the door.

The following Sunday she was back with us, and took her seat on my stool. I gave her healing for ten minutes. Then, as I took my hand away, her sight returned. She had a little weep, gave me a hug and a kiss, and then marched over to the donation box. Not for a quiet donation, but to address my wife.

"Your husband has just given me my sight back in my left eye. I'd like to place this in your donation tin as a thank you for what he has done." With that, she placed a fifty pence piece (.75 U.S.) in Kath's hand.

The price of sight! - less than a dollar! You can only be amazed at where people place their values.

An attitude of gratitude is a potent immunizer against many ills that befall us. Lack of appreciation for the gifts God gives us — and even for the trials (each one has a spiritual lesson within it) that life brings can deplete our own power to heal or be healed. In the Gospel of Luke (17:11-19), Jesus heals ten lepers, but of the ten, only one comes back to thank him. His soul had been reached. A truly healed spirit will also reflect qualities of gratitude and appreciation, if not for the healer, at least for the Source, which is God.

Yes, it is a funny old world. I went into my local pub one hot summer evening. Standing at the bar was the husband of a lady who had received instant relief from the acute pain she was suffering after a spinal operation. After weeks of almost unbearable agony, she received a healing on the very first visit.

"What would you like to drink?" he said as I approached the bar.

"Well, thank you, I'll have a pint of mild," I replied.

He looked me up and down. "I weren't talking to you!" he answered gruffly, "I were asking me mate over there, behind you."

Although I didn't get the pint, I learned a lesson. Never assume anything, even when it seems you have a right to.

THE POWER OF THE MEDIA

With Havercroft, the pressure was off my home life. I was still working six days a week at my building firm, and had resumed making home visits in the evenings in my Rolls.

"You think more of sick people than you do of us!" Adele, my eldest daughter yelled at me as I left the dinner table one night to give a healing in another village. By "us," of course, she meant Kath, Karl, Catherine and herself. "We can never go on picnics or have holidays like real families do," she protested.

"Honey," I answered, "I've always given you all you've ever asked for. I never refused you anything if it could be afforded." She was not appeased.

"It's not the same! We never go anywhere as a family!"

Adele was only nine years old, but she cut straight to the truth. I got the message and booked a two-week family holiday in Majorca. I brought along my healing request book and every night at 10 p.m. I went to my room and had ten minutes of prayer with the sick. It was a lovely break, we thoroughly enjoyed it and I found a new surge of energy within me. I needed it for what was about to come.

Only a day or two after our return, Dennis Thompson dropped by.

"Smithy! when you go down to the hall on Wednesday, be a good bloke, make sure you are looking smart, put a collar and tie on - and goodness sake get your hair cut!"

I just stared at him. "What's the big occasion? Is the Queen coming?"

"No! Yorkshire Television!"

"You're joking!"

"I'm not!"

"But what if the clients don't want to be interviewed?"

"Smithy, my old mate, while you were away, I've been busy. I've been in touch with scores of people, those who won't mind will be there. Don't worry about it - just be there!"

To be honest, I was terrified.

On Wednesday, the hall was transformed into something resembling Dante's inferno. Unless you've been to a studio and witnessed the organized chaos that prevails, it's hard to imagine the scene. Lights, the heat, a seemingly endless tangle of wires and cables, the dolly weaving in, back and around, carrying lights or cameras amidst conversations whirling about in a language only the unit crew could possibly understand.

"It's boomy!" shouts someone. Translation, the acoustics are prolonging power pitched sounds.

"Hit this with a snoot!" bellows another voice, and a grip adjusts a mask on one of the sizzling arc lamps.

The director issues instructions to everyone; the floor manager, microphone in hand, engages in conversations with half a dozen locations while the cameraman tracks around the scene on a dolly, or is perched precariously on the rostrum, checking his shots as riggers struggle to place their overhead lights to the satisfaction of the producer, director, and cameraman.

Then a single voice silences everything.

"O.K. we'll go for a take!" A sudden stillness fills the room, and here I am, caught in the middle. Suppose I froze! What sort of questions are they going to ask me? What if I say the wrong thing?

Robert Hall, the interviewer, held nothing back. He was playing the devil's advocate for his audience, which was all of Yorkshire. Fortunately, I knew my subject well.

"Tell me, what evidence is there to support this type of healing?"

"The evidence is the simple fact that people who were classed as incurable by the medical profession have been healed."

"In that case, could it not be a case of self suggestion?"

"If that's the case, then why hasn't the person's own doctor, or members of their family 'suggested' to them that they get better? And, how do you suggest to a baby, or a dog, or a horse, that they get well?" By now a great calmness had settled over me and I was feeling quite confident.

"If this kind of healing is as good as you claim, why do doctors laugh and sneer about it?"

"If doctors laugh and sneer, as you say, why do they send their patients along to us for treatment? If they laugh at healers, why do they come for Spiritual Healing — and bring their family members?"

"Are you implying that the medical profession has accepted Spiritual Healing?"

"No. Doctors are individuals, they have a right to their own views, but the acceptance is growing."

I reminded him that the General Medical Council in 1977 changed their policy regarding spiritual healers. Physicians were granted permission to suggest to their patients that they could seek help from a healer, providing the doctor retained complete charge of the case. Prior to this, doctors could be struck off the medical register for associating with healers.

Not to be appeased, he tried coming from another tact.

"You say that your healing powers come from God. There's a large number of scientists who would argue that these powers come from your subconscious mind. Whatever is being sent is transmitted to a patient from the healer's own brain. What do you say about that?"

"Quite simply this. The human brain, even the subconscious mind, cannot act upon knowledge it does not possess. If I say to that scientist, my television has broken down, repair it for me, and he has no knowledge or experience of television electronics, could he do it? I think not. I, Malcolm Smith, do not have the knowledge to heal the sick, to restore sight, to remove serious illnesses or disabilities. This healing power flows through me, not from me."

"Then where does it come from?"

"Wherever it comes from must have an unimaginable amount of knowledge and intelligence to overcome what appears to be impossible tasks - miracles, if you want to call them that. That somewhere, I believe, is from God. How could it be otherwise?"

Robert brought up some of my clients and interviewed them as well. The whole filming took over three hours. When the program aired two weeks later, it had been edited down to five minutes, and aroused enormous interest.

At the next clinic, three and four hundred people were lined up for healing. The Parish Hall was packed to capacity, standing room only. The hall looked like an overcrowded hospital admitting room. After waiting several hours, quite a number realized that it was impossible for everyone to be seen, and left for home.

Now here's the irony — while the TV show created enormous interest and I was the star of the broadcast, I couldn't share in the healing. The week before, I had seriously injured my hand doing construction work. It was a great embarrassment to be out of commission. Bill and Margaret Lloyd stepped in and did a marvelous job. In company with other healers, they all spent seven hours administering healing. All of them agreed that it was a day they will remember forever. One television appearance brought people to Havercroft from all over England. In twelve months we dealt with over five thousand people, many coming as a result of that TV screening.

WORLDWIDE RECOGNITION

It had only been a few years since the psychic lady told me I had a healing gift and would become "world famous." I could see I was certainly becoming well known in Yorkshire. Then, thanks to Dennis Thompson and the Robert Hall show, I was gaining a reputation throughout England. Dennis added to the effort by writing articles about the healings and sending them out to newspapers. The biggest, most widely distributed metaphysical newspaper in the world accepted one of his articles, and the psychic lady's prophecy was fulfilled.

His article in the "Psychic News" appeared in February 1984. Over the following weeks, hundreds of requests for absent healing poured in, with many asking for a healing handkerchief. I sent out hundreds throughout England, to America, Dubai, Sweden, Canada, Malaya and countries in the Far East.

Two weeks after the article appeared, a wire service that supplied stories to the news outlets worldwide sent a reporter to interview me. His article went out on the wire and was picked up by newspapers all over the world, including the National Inquirer, and another deluge of letters poured in from countries around the globe. A young woman in Dubai wrote saying she was devastated to learn from medical tests that she would never bear children of her own. She had read of my healing work in her local newspaper. I sent her absent healing and a handkerchief. Twelve weeks later she wrote me with a glowing testimonial, saying, after many years of barrenness, she was now pregnant. But even more important, she had also found God.

From the Middle East, a letter came from the mother of a seven-year-old boy who had been born with a withered hand. His father had taken their boy to specialists all over the world without any success. After reading of my healing powers, she nagged her husband into sending for one of my handkerchiefs. I sent the handkerchief with the instructions on how and when to apply it. A few weeks later, the boy's father wrote back saying that there had been a marked improvement in his son's condition - virtually overnight.

One lady in her middle sixties spent her life savings on a round trip fare from Florida to Heathrow. Surely, her angels were watching over her. When she arrived, all she had was her passport, a road map of Great Britain, her ticket home, and my address. She managed to hitch a ride with a long distance truck driver who lived only three miles from me. After her healing, the helpful driver invited her to stay with him and his family. A few days later he drove her back to London for her homeward flight.

People came from everywhere. They flew in from Sweden, Canada, and Malaya. They came without warning, without advance notice or any attempt to inform me of their intentions. They just turned up on my doorstep to ask for healing. No one was ever turned away.

THE END OF HAVERCROFT HALL

At Havercroft, I began to feel victimized by my own success. The hall was packed, and the lines extended out through the door, with people waiting as long as three hours to receive the healing. The long wait began generating a feeling of restlessness and frustration with many people. As a result, the atmosphere of the Sunday healing services started to decline. Instead of showing respect and reverence for the Spiritual Source, our clients fell out among themselves, disputing who was next in line. There were always some who insisted that they were first. I grew discouraged by the pettiness and constant complaints. To relieve the stress and prevent more arguments, we issued numbered tickets on arrival, but it did little or nothing to prevent line jumpers. We requested preference be granted to tiny babies, or that the cancer sufferers might have priority. Some hope! If ever there was an illustration of the worst side of human nature, this was it!

"What's the difference between her cancer pain and my bad back, eh?"

"It's all very well letting them kids in for treatment, what about my kids at home?"

Quite a number of our clients - mostly men, but some women - came straight from the pub, reeking of alcohol and speaking with slurred speech. I am no teetotaler. People can get drunk if they like, it's their choice, but it was unacceptable to me that they would come in that condition to a Spiritual Presence.

None of the healers were there for the money. Perhaps it was just as well, considering how many times we found aspirins, cigarette ends, plastic buttons and foreign coins in the collection box. The healing team made no demands or conditions for our visitors. We were there to heal. Perhaps that was the root of the problem. We had become part of the fixtures and fittings. Everyone just expected us to be there, no questions asked.

One Sunday we decided to have a fundraiser. Every penny we collected would go to the Andrew Hardwick Liver Fund. Andrew lived only a few miles from Havercroft. Bill and Margaret Lloyd, and myself, had gone every week for almost eighteen months to give him healing prior to his liver transplant. He was both a local and a national celebrity. We thought a fundraiser would generate a good response. There were close to one hundred people in the hall that day. Normally we could have expected about $30.00 in donations. We explained the purpose of the collection, expecting a substantial increase in donations. Instead we collected under $20.00! - less than a quarter per head!

Our Wednesday evening cancer clinic night had additional problems. We had to share a huge side room with local council members. A leather sliding partition separated us from each other. The council meetings grew very rowdy on occasion with raised voices and tables banged with gavels and fists. By contrast, on our side, we quietly asked our clients how they had been since their last visit and played soft, background music, such as Mantovani or Richard Clayderman - yet we were accused of being too noisy. One evening Bill Lloyd caught a councilor probing into our donation box. "I just wanted to see how much you've taken in," he said without a tinge of shame. Periodically, we had to do our healing work to the beat of a noisy disco. Trying to administer healing with Boy George belting out from half a dozen blasting loudspeakers was spirit deadening and virtually impossible.

The final straw came when a gentleman in his late sixties came into the hall and blamed me for his father's death. His 93-year-old father had died from pneumonia. He claimed it was the result of a cold he caught while waiting for healing in the Parish Hall. "But your father also had cancer in both lungs," I answered. It did nothing to pacify him, and it pushed me over the top. I was through.

I asked the other healers if they would like to carry on running the Wednesday and Sunday clinics. No one stepped forth. It was over. After nearly sixteen months, the healing services at Havercroft Parish Hall, which had attracted people from all over England, finally came to an end.

My first five years of healing had its share of heartache and hardship. I never asked for, wanted or expected fame or fortune, but I did expect respect, not for myself, but for the Source - God.

Two lessons were soon learned from the hall. The first was that the people who regularly attended my home and readily accepted free treatment and refreshments never came near the hall. I wondered why? Second, with a donation box I thought we could at least cover the cost of renting the premises. Wrong. More often than not, the rent came out of my pocket. 'Thanks for the memory and making me better, pal! Here's a cigarette butt for your donation tin!' The spectacle of selfishness and ingratitude cut like a knife.

Tommy Smith was right when he said that wherever I went with my gift of healing, it would be a hard road to travel. How right he was. There is a price to be paid for healing - and I wondered, who pays it, the healed, or the healer?

Still, the experience of working at Havercroft Hall, of meeting new faces, of witnessing the healing and relief of those who came in pain and suffering, seeing their astonishment as the conditions were removed or alleviated, brought great joy. It's an experience I wouldn't trade for the Queen's jewels.

CHAPTER SIX

FULL TIME, BAD TIMES

The long lines and declining conditions discouraged many ill and suffering people from coming to Havercroft. There was a demand and a need for healing, yet those who were in the most distress and pain found it too difficult to continue. The construction business was prospering. We stayed very busy and were making good money. My house was paid off and I was debt free. But I wasn't satisfied. My heart was with the healing work. It was my passion. Until I could put all my energies into healing, I would never be at peace. A bigger hall with a seven-day schedule, I decided, would eliminate the problems we experienced at Havercroft.

I went to my partner with a proposition.

"Ray," I said, "if I can make a go of healing full time, then I'm willing to give you my half of the construction business free and clear." Ray clearly was interested, and listened intently to my only condition. "I'm only asking that while I'm testing it out, Ray, you provide the means to support me and family over the next six months. This will give me the opportunity to go into healing full time, and a way back, in case it doesn't work out."

Ray agreed. I drove over to Wakefield, about ten miles from Ryhill, and found a grand old Victorian house for rent. I felt it would make a great clinic. In February 1984 I signed a 5-year lease, and felt primed and ready to begin my new career. I couldn't have made a bigger mistake at a worse time. Less than a month after I signed the lease, the miners went on strike over the conditions in mines. The miners' union was the strongest union in the nation. Earlier walkouts had toppled two previous Conservative governments. Prime Minister Thatcher wasn't about to let it happen to her and she shut down the mines. Her public statement was that they weren't making a profit. Her real reason was to break the miners' union. By closing down the mines, she would eliminate the threat to her power.

The strike lasted for one year, and brought the whole economy to a standstill. As the strike went on conditions steadily worsened. Bread lines and soup kitchens became common. Riots broke out, and many businesses — some over 120 years old — went belly up. When it was over, the miners won nothing, and many of the mines never re-opened.

From March through Christmas, the first nine months of the twelve-month strike, Nat West bank continued to encourage us to borrow money to complete new homes. They assured us that it was only going to be "a few more weeks and the strike would be over." In truth, after the first six months of the strike people were not buying new houses, they were not even spending money on their existing properties.

By September and October, the effects of the miners' strike were being felt throughout the country. Negotiations with the government continued, but with little evidence of progress. As the holidays drew near, conditions grew bleaker. People were selling their furniture, piece by piece, to meet their mortgage demands, and selling their cars to keep food on the table. Then just before Christmas Nat West raised up the ghost of old Scrooge and shut off our credit line. At that time we owed something in the region of $150,000, plus the accruing interest, mounting up at an alarming rate each day.

With our firm headed toward the rocks, I felt I had offended God because of the Rolls Royce. The Rolls had seduced me. I had worked hard for four years to buy it. To me it had been a talisman; bulletproof insurance against disaster. Now, on the verge of bankruptcy, I felt shamed by my "Roller." To me, it had simply inflated my ego and shriveled my soul. To make amends with God and to ease my conscience, I told Ray I was going to donate the Rolls to a children's charity. Ray wouldn't hear of it.

"No," he said firmly. "The Rolls is a tangible asset, if we lose it, we won't be able to borrow so easily and keep the business afloat."

The downturn in our business continued relentlessly. Eventually, I sold the Rolls for $7,500 less than I paid for it three years before. The money went back into the business, and things kept getting worse.

The strike finally ended in March of 1985. Margaret Thatcher crushed the miners' union. The miners won absolutely nothing and lost a great deal of power. The effects of the strike were disastrous throughout the mining areas. No one was buying houses any more; those who had bought them were struggling to survive the mortgage demands. We had uncompleted houses and perpetual expenses to face. Everyone was crippled in some way, and I was feeling the pain.

Even so, there was one little bizarre incident that even now brings a smile to my face. Gilbert Tile, the head manager at Nat West bank, called for a meeting with my partner, Raymond, and myself to discuss our indebtedness. We arranged to meet at Ray's house. Ray's wife, Matilda, made coffee for us.

"Stand up, Malcolm," Mr. Tile ordered, after finishing his coffee. "Right here, in front of me."

"Right!" I said. He extended his hand toward me. "Try squeezing it as hard as you can." I took his hand and gripped it firmly. "Harder!" he persisted, "as if you were trying to break it."

Ray stood behind him, mouthing a silent message. "Go on, Malc! Break his fingers!"

Still gripping his fingers hard, I asked sheepishly, "Why do you want me to try and break your hand?"

"Just keep squeezing. When I tell you, just let go of my wrist and give me your hand, palm up."

Well, anything to please a bank manager. I added more pressure to my grip. "Stop," he said and I showed him my hand. He started examining my palm.

"What are you doing with my hand?"

"I read palms for a hobby," he answered without looking up. "Nearly went doing it full time a few years ago." Couldn't see any future in it, I thought!

He stared at my hand and searched among the lines for several minutes. Finally, with a serious look on his face, he announced, "Malcolm! You are a very nervous person!" I waited for more, but that was it. Ray put his hand to his mouth to stifle his laughter. We owed the bank $150,000. That was enough to make anybody nervous!

"Right, Ray! Your turn!" Mr. Tile grabbed his hand and began looking intently at Ray's palm. "Ray, I'm afraid you are going to have to work very hard for a living for the rest of this life."

"How does he know that?" Ray asked me later.

"It's flaming obvious, isn't it. We'll both have to work eighteen hours a day, seven days a week for the next ninety years to pay back all we owe."

"Would you read my palm, please?" Ray's wife said, extending her hand. Mr. Tile took her discretely into another room for a private reading. Matilda came out ashen faced and glum.

"What did he tell you?" Ray asked after Mr. Tile left.

"He said I was going to die as soon as I reach pensionable age."

I grimaced. How could a man who was in charge of a large bank be so thoughtless! Was he as equally tactless with the bank's employees?

"What is the age of retirement for women?" Matilda's tone was somber. Clearly, she was upset.

"Sixty!" I answered.

"Well, that's not too bad, I still have twenty-three years to go!"

"Yeah, but what happens if they lower the retirement age?" Ray jibbed.

Matilda's eyes filled with tears. Good old Ray! He certainly knew how to upset his wife.

"It's all a load of rubbish," I said, and spent the next half hour trying to console her.

NO MORE FREE SERVICE — AT WHAT COST!

My healing work was costing me a lot of money to carry on. The weekly rent itself was a huge part of the overhead. Against my strongly held principles, I realized I would have to request a modest charge for healing, even for the pensioners. But at what level should I set the fee? No matter what price, many elderly people would not be able to afford it. To make it easier for them and to insure they get the help they needed, I decided pensioners could get free treatment on Saturdays, — and what a pattern emerged! People, quite obviously not of pensionable age, immediately began showing up for free treatments. Predictably, the results were disastrous!

On the first free Saturday, one immaculately dressed, very well spoken couple arrived. The lady limped badly from a severe pain in her right knee. "I've had this pain for months," she explained as I sat her down in a chair, and placed my hands on her knee. The healing had an immediate effect. Her response was spontaneous. She hugged and kissed me while her husband looked on completely unmoved.

I freed myself from her embrace, and went to the cupboard to get her a handkerchief for distant healing. While I rummaged through the box, I heard her whisper hoarsely to her husband, "Have you put anything in the box?"

"I've put a pound in," he replied.

"Put another pound in."

"A pound is enough!"

She took the handkerchief, thanked me once again for her 'miracle' and they left. I stood at the window and watched as they drove away in a brand new $15,000 Saab Turbo. Yet a pound was enough.

Another of those young looking 'pensioners' who had been a regular over the weeks, always repaid my treatment with the sum of a nickel. One week she told me she would not be coming the following Saturday.

"You won't?"

"No, sonny, you see it's my turn for week end work — Oh!" Her hand covered her mouth as the truth slipped out. Although she was supposed to be a pensioner, she just confessed to having a job. Her face went bright red. She turned on her heel and rushed out of the clinic. I never saw her again.

A few days later I had a telephone call from a coal miner asking if he could bring his wife for healing.

"Of course you can," I assured him.

"I can't pay you 'owt pal, I'm on strike!"

I thought it over for a moment.

"What exactly is wrong with your wife?" I asked.

"Depression."

"Could you put your wife on the phone so that I can talk to her?"

"Sorry mate, she don't get home from work until half past eight tonight."

I suggested he could get his wife to call me the following day.

"Sorry mate, she works six days a week in the supermarket."

"Yet you can't pay me anything?"

"Well no, I told you, I'm on strike."

"Does your wife work for nowt?" I asked.

"Does she heck as like work for nowt!" he responded aggressively.

"Neither do I pal!" and I slammed the phone down. It was the first time I was offhand with a caller. But I was fed up, angry, and buried in debt, and no one, not even God, seemed to care.

Another time, a lady telephoned me for an appointment. She had been a regular at Havercroft and had only just found out about my Wakefield address.

"Oh it will be just like old times again," she enthused.

"Well not quite," I replied, "you see I am obliged to charge, but only $7.00 for people of pensionable age."

She went up the wall.

"Malcolm Smith! I never thought I would ever see the day when you would charge money for healing."

I tried to explain but she cut me off. "Healing comes from God! How dare you charge anything for something that doesn't belong to you!"

I tried to explain the rent alone was almost $150 a week, with lighting, heating, phone bills and other expenses added. "God does not provide a weekly check to meet these items."

"Don't try and wangle your way out of this!" she shouted over the phone. "He feeds the birds of the air doesn't He?"

"They are starving in Ethiopia," I reminded her.

"My God!" she said with disgust. The phone went dead.

And there were the people who showed no appreciation, even when their loved ones received help or were healed.

A lady who came to Wakefield for contact healing for her arthritis added her grandson's name to my absent healing list. The boy was nine years old and had not spoken a recognizable word since birth.

"All he can say are garbled noises that no one can understand. Not even his special ed teachers know what he's trying to say."

After two weeks of absent healing, the lad began to talk. Grandma was filled with joy! In her excitement, she blurted out to the parents that she had asked for healing for him, but had not dared to tell them until now.

"It's only been two weeks and he's speaking! It's a miracle!" she proclaimed.

"Healing my foot!" the dad responded. "The lad's nine years old, it's only time he started talking!"

If you can't appreciate the power of prayer, I thought, at least give thanks to God!

All through this time I felt sorely tested. To be a healer you have to have an inner feeling for people, to want to help and ease their suffering any way you can. It really comes down to this: how much love and compassion do you have for your fellow man? With love, compassion and the desire to heal, anyone can be a healer. It's like singing. It's an innate ability within all of us that increases with practice and experience. But if you don't have love and compassion, you won't develop at a deep level. Love, compassion, and forgiveness, these were my most challenging lessons.

FORECLOSURE

It was storming outside. Ray and I sat in silence listening to the rain beating steadily on the leaded glass windows of the living room. Usually in the spring, the building trade enjoys a flourish with people requiring additions, renovations, maybe a brick garage, or new garden walls. There was nothing anywhere.

"So you've no work in the pipeline?" I asked.

"With a bit of luck there may be some in April," Ray answered.

Sure enough, the first week of April we got our 'bit of luck.' It amounted to a few small jobs, laying some brick and minor home improvements, and our work soon ran out. Eight weeks later Ray and I received letters from Nat West ordering us to put our houses up for sale, with all the proceeds from the sale going to the bank. In other words, we were about to be homeless. I was shattered. How could this be happening to me!

For 20 years, I had worked hard and saved to pay off my mortgage. I didn't owe a single penny to anyone for it. For the past five years, the sick, the lame, and the dying had come to me. I had given myself over to healing, charging little or nothing for God's work to be done. Sure I had made mistakes, but doesn't God have mercy? And what about my wife and family? What's to happen to them?

My lawyer said there was absolutely nothing I could do. I had used my house as collateral against the borrowing. The bank was now the owner.

Desperate times call for desperate measures. My home meant everything to me. I had always been the provider, the support for my family. I was boiling with rage. If God was being silent on this, then it was up to me. I wasn't going down without a fight, and I came out swinging.

Our neighbors next door suddenly put their house up for sale. We needed a roof over our heads. Although it was only a two-bedroom house, I decided to take out a mortgage and buy it. I went to our accountant and asked him to fix the books so we could get a loan.

"But you don't have the numbers," he said.

"That's what I mean — fix the books to show we do!"

My intensity overrode any objections he might dare to raise. I meant what I said, and he knew it. He adjusted the figures, and the loan went through.

My partnership with Ray was only nominal by now. It was a cloudy, dark, stormy day as I headed out to find him, to see if he could find work for me. The weather felt ominous and oppressive, as bleak and foul as my prospects.

"I'm sorry, mate, I have no work either," he replied. My spirit sank. That which I was fighting against was greater than I.

From the beacon of light it first seemed to be, the clinic in Wakefield was now a crippling burden. The weekly rent and overhead was burying me. I went to the landlord and pleaded my case. He was unmoved.

"You signed a 5-year contract, and you'll stick to it. I'll see that you do!"

In some ways, losing everything can free you. Now that my home was gone, I had nothing more to lose. If he wanted to sue me there wasn't much left he could take. I decided to test his will. I figured he had no grudge against me personally; all he wanted was his rent. It didn't matter whose pocket it came from, as long as the rent was paid. We met several times, and eventually we reached a win-win arrangement. I would continue to pay the rent while he would do his utmost to try to find a buyer.

A number of weeks passed before a prospective buyer appeared. Clark Mayfield was a dentist, and he was impressed with the building. Due to the strained economy, the price of the building was low — it could be bought as an investment — and it suited his needs as a dentist. There was only one snag. He was on the fence about continuing his practice. He had been in constant pain for several months with a severe back problem. Dr. Clark had tried all types of treatment, from the orthodox to osteopaths without success. The pain was forcing him to consider early retirement.

"Have you ever tried Spiritual Healing?" I asked.

"It's about the only thing I haven't tried," he answered. For Clark, like many of the people who come to see me, Spiritual Healing is the court of last resort. It is only after they've tried everything else and given up hope that they are willing to try something as unorthodox and unconventional as spirit-guided healing.

During the first session, with some astonishment, Dr. Clark said my hands were radiating soothing warmth like a heating pad and he felt tingling throughout his body. His pain diminished considerably. By the fourth session, his problem totally cleared up and he purchased the clinic and continued his practice for many years. For him, Wakefield became a sound and profitable investment. On the other hand, my twelve months at the clinic incurred a loss of over ten thousand dollars.

Still, I felt a great sadness on the day I moved out of my Bond Street Healing Sanctuary. In spite of all the misery and the anxieties, I still honestly believed the Wakefield Clinic had been heaven sent for me to do God's work here on earth. I stood on the street, reflecting back over those twelve months. I could recall the good days and the many 'characters' that came for healing. The Brigadier General from Malaysia came to mind and the three Arabs in long flowing gowns, who made a special journey from London after hearing of my services. They might have donated an oil well, I thought wryly. Instead they chipped in together and deposited the princely sum of a fiver in the donation box.

I felt great satisfaction with the many healing successes at Wakefield, especially the two that gave me a way to silence my critics. The first case involved a three-year-old filly named Dancer. Dancer appeared to be dying. Her jaw had become paralyzed after tearing open her mouth on a gate, and she was unable to eat. Joan Outwood, the mother of the horse's owner, phoned me and requested healing prayer for Dancer. I immediately responded with distant healing and began sending energy to the horse. Dancer was fully cured — virtually overnight — and was soon cantering around her paddock, fully fit.

The second case concerned a Jack Russell terrier named Beauty. Beauty had fallen hard from the bed of a truck and landed on her head, severely injuring her neck. Joyce and Henry Johnson, her owners, took Beauty to the vet and were told she was only badly bruised and the condition would clear up. After three months of terrible pain, lots of medication, x-rays and injections, Beauty was decidedly worse. The Johnsons were advised that their prized dog had a calcified disc. An operation might ease the pain, but leave her with a permanently stiff neck. Even worse, she could be paralyzed. The Johnsons called for an appointment, and brought her in to see me. Beauty was a very obedient dog and a joy to work on. She sat quietly on the floor, panting, with her face tilted toward me while I put my hands on her neck and asked for healing. The answer came instantly. Beauty was completely cured. From this one visit, all signs of stiffness and pain vanished.

It satisfied me to know that the hardest cynic could not challenge the power or source of the healing force by dismissing it as 'suggestion.' How do you 'suggest' to a horse or a dog that they are healed!

These reflections were a moment of calm while all around me the storm clouds were gathering. I walked away from the clinic with no idea what lay ahead. I may well have collapsed if I did.

IT GETS WORSE BEFORE IT GETS BETTER

In July, 1985, the next blow hit. It was midday Friday. The family and I were eating our lunch when there was a knock at the back door. I opened the door to a middle aged man with a briefcase. Thinking he was here for healing, I said, "Come on in and take a chair. I'll be with you in a minute."

"Take a chair?" he said. "I'm coming for the whole lot." I blinked, not comprehending.

He produced an official looking sheet of paper and waved it in my face. "Do you want to discuss things on the door step for everyone to hear or shall I come inside?"

Our building firm was now defunct but still had outstanding debts. Two local suppliers had sent this bailiff with a court order to possess pieces of furniture to settle their unpaid bills. The bailiff made his way through our three small downstairs rooms, itemizing the contents on his notepad.

"If you can't pay me now, I'll be back for the furniture with a truck before evening." He motioned, pointing to the table where my wife and children still sat, with their food untouched. "And this will be the first to go." The children became frightened, and started crying and wailing. Kathleen reached out and pulled Catherine and Karl to her, trying to comfort them, but her eyes stayed fixed on the bailiff. Instinctively, Adele went to her mother and stood next to her. When the bailiff threatened to pull up the room carpet as well if we couldn't make a payment, Kath became hysterical.

"Malc, do something," she pleaded. "Don't let him do this!" My family was shocked and in tears. The only money I could spare was the cash we had put aside for the electric bill. I offered the utility money, but it wasn't enough. I rushed from the house over to my cousin who lived on the row several doors down and borrowed the rest from them. After the debt was paid, the bailiff produced a form that stated I would not dispose of any furniture until all the firm's debts had been paid - and insisted I sign it.

With no money left to pay for our electricity, the power was cut off, and I was forced to borrow from family members again. This was just the beginning. On average, the bailiffs came once a month to recover debts of our now defunct building firm. Sometimes the older men were compassionate and understanding, but some of the younger ones seemed to exult in their power and our misfortune. In England, bailiffs are not simply bill collectors, they carry the backing of the government with them — and some parade their authority and wield it with impunity and arrogance. One came in, sipping on a coke bottle. When he finished his drink, he set the bottle on the window ledge and continued inspecting the house. When he was ready to leave, I reminded him to take his bottle with him.

"I'll leave it for you," he sneered. "Use the deposit toward your debt."

I felt my stomach turn sour with a rush of depression, guilt and anger, shamed by the humiliation and powerless to retaliate.

In the village, signs of Christmas began to appear as the season drew nearer. I dreaded each day. I knew this Christmas would be the worst one we had ever known. Other parents were busy buying and wrapping toys for their children, while our kids were going to their little friends, trying to sell their toys to ease our misfortune. Adele sold her majorette's baton and gave us the money to buy food over the holiday season. Catherine sold several of her dolls, and Karl, who was very quiet and kept to himself, even went out and sold some of his precious toy soldiers and metal cars. Although they were only children, they understood what a financial nightmare we were going through. When Christmas day arrived, there was little to celebrate — except that the holy season seemed to keep the bill collectors at bay.

The first three months of the New Year saw a renewal of activity by the bailiffs. On one occasion I was threatened with prison for selling a piece of furniture to buy some groceries. I was now out of work, trying to keep my family fed and incoming bills paid on $70 per week from the government.

I didn't think things could get any bleaker, but the pressure continued to mount. Kath's grandmother died very suddenly. She was a wonderful old lady and a dear, close friend to Kath. Karl had his trail bike stolen; Catherine's pet cat was run over, and I became quite ill, suffering with nervous depression. Finally, Kath cracked under the tremendous pressures with a nervous breakdown. One of the things that Tommy Smith had told me when I was first healing at Normanton was, "Life is a school, and the lessons are hard. If they don't kill you, they'll make you stronger." I was determined to get stronger.

The first thing I did when that black Christmas was over was to start work on the house at 39 Mill Lane. Only a few weeks before I took out the mortgage for the house, the old lady living next door died quite suddenly after a short illness. It had been my Dad's house, and he had left it to me. After his death I had rented it out to the now deceased tenant. I got the idea of knocking out the common wall shared by the two houses, and making it a larger, family house. I had no spare cash for the project, but being in the building trade I did a lot of the work myself. When I needed help, my friends who were tradesmen gave me a hand.

Around 5:30 one evening a representative from Nat West knocked on the door. Our psychic bank manager, Mr. Tile, sent him to inquire if anyone had been interested in buying No. 41. When I told him no, he asked if he could have a look around No. 37.

"Why?" I asked.

"Because the bank owns it now."

"That house was left to me by my father!" I protested.

"Yes, Mr. Smith, and you signed it over as security two years ago. It's our house now," he answered in a clipped, cold and measured voice. I was stunned. In the crush of events I had pushed aside that fact from my memory. I had completely forgotten. We walked the short distance from 41 to 37. I was in a kind of semi-daze as I unlocked the door and switched on the light.

"What on earth have you done?" His eyes were ready to pop their sockets. I had torn out everything, leaving only the bare shell of the rooms.

"I'm making the two units into one," I explained.

"It looks like a bomb's gone off here!"

"The conversion work is only just started."

"What on earth is Mr. Tile going to say when I tell him what you've done to our property?"

"It is not yours, it's mine!" I insisted blindly as the agent walked away.

Two days later Mr. Tile sent a letter requesting an interview with me regarding the property. He insisted I restore the house to its original condition. Knowing it would take several thousands of pounds to do that, I made an offer to buy it back from the bank — or rather, buy it back from myself — for half its market value. Reluctantly the bank agreed, but before the building society allowed me the advance, all the work on the house had to be completed. I was caught in a Catch 22. The trauma was unbearable. "If it doesn't kill you, it makes you stronger." I wasn't sure I could make it through this lesson.

By July we found a buyer for 41 Mill Lane. It was a young family with two small children. They were due to move in on the 22nd of the month, and 37/39 was nowhere near completed. The bank relented a little and offered me one thousand pounds out of the sale of 41. I had sold the unit 41 completely furnished, carpets, light fixtures, stove and all the utilities included. In other words, I now had money to complete the renovations at 37/39, but nowhere to live and no furniture.

Eventually my father's sister, Aunt Ethel, shared her home with us. Kath and I slept in her bedroom with Karl. Our girls shared the guest room, and Aunt Ethel slept on the sofa downstairs. The Smith clan is a large family, and we help each other. Not once did Aunt Ethel make us feel we were imposing on her. The money provided by the bank, along with aid from the local Department of Social

Services, gave us the means to make 37/39 habitable. It took six months before we could move in. God bless Aunt Ethel!

CHAPTER SEVEN

THE END OF HEALING, A CHANGE OF HEART

Word traveled through the shire and beyond that we were down and nearly out. Yet no one came with help. Looking back now, I understand many of my neighbors and people throughout the region were feeling the effects of the strike. But at the time, I was drowning in my own problems, and angry with everyone, including God. All during this time, when I had no work, no home, hardly any furniture, and not even two pennies to rub together, out of the many thousands of people I had helped over the years, no one stepped in to help me —not even from the Spiritualist Church, where I had donated so much time and effort. Only Bill and Izzy Donaldson and Mary and Dennis Thompson came near to see how we were. I felt very bitter indeed; my anger slowly turned into a depression so bleak and numbing that I started sleeping sixteen hours a day, refusing to see anyone.

Once word got round that I was back in the village, people started knocking on my door asking for healing. These were people I had treated before, and who had ignored me when I had no means of helping them. On most days, I was too paralyzed to get out of bed. Kath had the unhappy task of turning them away. Even newcomers who were hearing about my work and coming for the first time were refused. On the rare days when I answered the door, I told them I didn't do healing anymore and sent them to the Spiritualist Church. Some pleaded that they had driven long distances to see me. "You should have phoned first," I told them, "instead of just showing up at my door." Everyone was denied!

Why should I help them? They didn't help me.

What right had they to clamor for my help when they wouldn't give anything in return?

Why had I spent so much time healing others, and so little paying attention to my business?

Why had I become so obsessed with healing that my family was suffering because of it?

There was something inside me deep, bottomless and dark, where everything was decaying and falling in on itself. I felt like I was back in the mines again, 3,000 feet below sunlight and fresh breezes, in that labyrinth of chiseled, tortured tunnels, with no miner's lamp for this deep hole, feeling isolated and remote from any source of healing or love. I had just let things go on, playing the selfless, healing hero to the masses. But even then, unknown to me, a slow mending process, barely noticeable at first, was beginning.

THE HAND OF GOD

No matter how far down we get, it's never so deep that God can't reach us. A friend of mine who was a contractor had, on a few occasions, some odd jobs to give me. It was very sporadic, but it was enough to keep me from feeling totally disillusioned with my life. My friend got a contract to do improvements on a big old home, and had subcontracted with a bunch of tradesmen, including myself. I was working at the site one day when I spied a glint in the grass where the men had been working all day. Curious, I went to see what it was. Lying in the grass attached to a bootlace was a brand new looking silver charm. It was in the image of an open hand. The effect it produced as I picked it up is hard to explain. It felt like a message, that this healing hand was meant for me, an assurance from the spirit world. Was it a healing hand? The hand of peace? An assurance that God's hand was still on my shoulder? I knew if anybody else picked it up, it wouldn't mean anything at all. But for me, in my circumstances, it meant a great deal.

I showed the necklace to every worker on the site and asked if they had dropped it. No one had.

"Malc, this is a message for you," said one of the men who knew about my work as a healer.

"Do you think so?" I answered, a bit surprised. Had he read my mind?

"I don't know what the message is," he continued, "but it's a message."

I wasn't sure what the message was, but the effect was immediate. It lifted me from my despair and hopelessness for many weeks, and then it slipped from my mind as my problems continued to mount.

THE GARDEN

Kath recovered from her breakdown, and on rare occasions when we had a couple of pounds to spare after paying our debts, we invested in packets of flower seeds or a few plants from the garden center. Our garden was very small, but the many hours we spent amidst the roses, the peonies, lilies and petunias with their multicolored faces and fragrances were deeply healing. Indeed, as one of our poets said, man is closer to God in a garden than anywhere else on earth. By now I was spending more time in the garden than I was in bed. My own healing was in the hands of the flowers.

After being sick and receiving benefits for almost six months, my health improved to the point where the Department of Social Services sent me for a medical examination. I was pronounced physically fit to start work. But there was a problem. No one I knew in Yorkshire was hiring forty-year-old laborers, and that's all I was — I had no trade as it were.

I was told to apply for welfare, and remain on the dole until I found employment. I thought it would be comparatively easy to find work. Wrong! Wrong! Wrong! It was another soul destroying experience filling out applications, only to be told that you are too old, or that you do not have the qualifications they need, or, as in many cases, the applicant doesn't even receive the courtesy of a reply. Job hunting was made more difficult by the fact that I had to sell my old mini car to pay a water bill.

It was strange indeed the day after I sold my car to be standing, waiting for a bus to take me to the Job Center. I couldn't recall when I had last ridden a bus, but I could remember the way I felt, just a short time ago, driving my own metallic Silver Shadow Rolls Royce! It is peculiar how short the distance can be between two extremes.

After Raymond and I sold our homes, our debt was reduced from $120,000 to $45,000, yet we were still standing in the long shadow of the bank. We had no other means for repaying the remainder, which was now comprised mainly of the interest that had accumulated over the years. In the background was always the possibility that the bank might force me to sell my present home.

A movie came out about this time, called 'Resurrection.' It was about a woman who was very gifted as a healer, but when a fanatic tried to kill her it all got too overwhelming. She escaped from her ministry by going to work in a small, broken down filling station in the middle of a desert in the western United States. I often wished there was a desert like that in Yorkshire, and I could vanish into it.

A medium told me that throughout this ordeal I had been through 'a trial by fire.' By now my healing practice had diminished by one hundred per cent. Finally, I resolved - "if it's been a trial by fire, then let fire be the end of it!" On Guy Fawkes Night, when bonfires and fireworks are lit throughout England in memory of our country's most famous traitor, I gathered everything I had left that was associated with my healing work - the sign up sheets, the distant healing request book, all my books about healing, even the healing stool the people sat on - and built my own bonfire with them in my back yard. It was over! I had received so little help for myself - why should I even consider helping others! It went to God as well. Why should I do God's work if God wouldn't step in and help me!

For the next two years I refused healing to everyone — including myself!

BABY KATIE

One of the great mysteries regarding healing — and one that often makes me shake my fist at God, is what I call the paradox of who gets healed. I have been called in to heal elderly people with serious illnesses, and they will get years added to their lives. At other times, I will treat young children and infants, sometimes with conditions that are minor or not considered life threatening, and others who have cancer, AIDS and other fatal diseases ... and they will not respond. Some have died. Why years should be added on to one who has lived a full lifetime, and life taken from a baby who has a whole lifetime before them, is a paradox I can't resolve.

It says in the Scripture, "A little child shall lead them." And it was one such child, a newborn baby with scarcely a hope of survival, that led me back on the path to what my soul so deeply loved, and began my own healing process. Indeed baby Katie's healing would set a chain of events in motion over the next nine years that would lead me to one of the greatest healers of the 20th Century and take me to America.

In May of 1987, my friends Bill and Isobel Donaldson drove up from their home in Brierley to ask if I could help a friend of theirs who was badly in need of aid. His name was Roche Bentley. His wife, Tricia, had given birth to a baby girl a few days earlier. Baby Katie, as they had named her, had been born with a hole in her heart, twisted heart valves and other serious complications. The surgeons had performed an immediate corrective surgery, but the baby was growing weaker by the day. Another surgery was planned, yet the surgeons believed Katie was not strong enough to survive a lengthy operation. It was all that they could do. There was little hope for baby Katie's survival.

Bill and Isobel asked if I would go down to Great Ormond Street Children's Hospital in London, where the baby was in intensive care.

"I don't do healing anymore. England's full of healers," I snapped. "Why don't you call one of them?"

"But they want you," Bill said. "I've told them all about you."

Bill persisted, and reluctantly I agreed. We hopped in his prized M.G. and drove down to London, arriving at midnight on Saturday. Katie was in an incubator. Tricia, her mother, was sitting on a chair at her baby's side, looking weepy eyed and strained.

I spent about ten minutes administering the healing energy to the infant, and told Roche if the healing was going to work, little Katie would improve enough by Wednesday for the needed surgery. The ward sister was present when I gave him this information.

Tricia looked exhausted, so I offered to give her healing, and she accepted. I sat her in a chair in the intensive care ward, and her husband and some of the nursing staff observed as I gave her a treatment. It was now 12:45 a.m. Sunday. Bill and I bid the Bentleys farewell and left the ward. We had not gone twenty yards when Roche came running after us.

"Malc! Tricia is crying her eyes out, she can't stop herself!"

"Don't try and stop her, Roche, it is all the stress leaving her. She will be great tomorrow, just you wait and see."

He smiled, "And what about Katie?"

I closed my eyes, half in tiredness, half in deep thought. "Wednesday, Roche, she'll be well enough by Wednesday."

Roche walked me to the car, and thanked me again for making the long trip to see his dying child. He reached in his pocket, and brought out a handful of pound notes. It was the equivalent of about $500.

"Here," he said … "please take this."

"No thanks," I said.

"It's ok," he responded. "I can afford it."

Several of the bills bore large denominations. I was sorely tempted. I was still out of work and in debt. But this was God's work, not mine.

"I don't take money from the rich or the poor for healing."

Roche looked at me in disbelief. "Well, I'll tell you what I'll do. If my daughter lives, I will publish a book about you and any stories of healing you may wish to include."

I had lots of stories to tell, but my education had stopped at age 15, and I was no author. I thought it was a fine offer, but who is going to write it? I wouldn't even know where to begin.

He thanked me again and Bill and I set off on our long journey north. On the way back, Bill told me about his friend. Roche Bentley was the owner of England's famous M.G. Sports Car owners club, a multimillionaire with access to his own publishing firm. Bill was excited by the idea of a book of healing stories. But I kept the same thought. Who's going to write it? Me? Now that would be a miracle in itself.

I tumbled into bed around 4:30 am. When I awoke, sometime in the mid afternoon, my thoughts went out to the Bentleys. Had I been clairvoyant when I told him that she would be all right by

Wednesday, or was it wishful thinking? Why hadn't I kept my mouth shut? They do say - whoever 'they' are - if in doubt, say nowt!

I need not have worried. On Monday the baby started gaining strength, its vital signs improved and its color returned. Tuesday, the improvements continued, and by the predicted day of Wednesday, the baby had made such a remarkable improvement that the surgeons were able to operate. It was a total success. The surgeons couldn't get over how fast she improved in such a short time, when in fact, they originally had predicted baby Katie had only a 5% chance of surviving the surgery. After surgery, they were equally amazed at the speed at which the baby made her recovery. Perhaps someone should tell them about Spiritual Healing, I thought.

And Tricia? Well, after she had that good cry, she went to lie down on a bed provided for parents of seriously ill children and had the best night's sleep for quite a long time. She felt 'marvelous' when she awoke.

And me? What did I get out of it? Well, it taught me that after two years of rebelling against God, the power was still there, as strong as ever — and I had to face myself in a different light. Someone once said that we should all be ashamed to die unless we have each achieved some great service for mankind. There was a time when I thought I was in the clear, but now, I had my doubts. I felt that all I had achieved as a healer had been wiped out by my selfish attitude these past two years, when I turned away people coming to me for help. My head hung low as I wondered how it would be if I were suddenly called Home, and had to account for myself to God and all the spirit guides and healers who had worked with me. Yet, again, I knew also that I had been fighting a great war within myself. I knew that I was sorely wounded, and for a while I believed it might have been fatal. But now, I knew I was recovering. My healing began with baby Katie.

GOD WORKS IN STRANGE WAYS

There's an old saying, "Your arms are too short to box with God." My anger was too hard to live with, and I missed the joy and satisfaction I received from healing work. My rebellious pouting made me as bad and shallow as the ones I had criticized for falsely professing to be my friends. If things were ever going to improve, I needed to lift myself above my judgments and self-condemnation and get back to work.

To begin, I went to the bookstore and bought a notebook. It had always been my practice to write down the names of the people I am praying for, the condition they want healed, and their physical location. On the first page of my new prayer request book, I carefully wrote baby Katie as the first entry at the top of the page, and resolved that whoever came to my door for healing, I would invite them in and do with my whole heart and soul what I was put on this earth to do.

Two days later Alan and Agnes Bottomley from Padiham in Lancashire came seeking my help. Our house was meagerly furnished, with some rooms bare, uncarpeted and unpainted. We had no stove, only one small microwave for cooking and heating water for tea. The renovations were far from finished. When the Bottomleys saw the mess we were still living in, they took it in their hearts to help. On their next visit, they came with a food hamper. They were the first to offer help, a couple on social security, who had little to spare. Kath and I were very touched and soon the Bottomleys became part of our family circle.

I added their names under baby Katie's in my prayer book. Alan added another name, Jack Summers, and requested absent healing for his friend. Jack was seventy years old and, for the past five months, suffered daily excruciating pain from chronic osteoarthritis in both hips. His condition was becoming progressively worse. Walking short distances was a painful, difficult task and Jack had also developed a noticeable limp.

I promised Alan that I would include his friend in my absent healing prayers that night. As an afterthought I "energized" a handkerchief for Alan to give to Jack with instructions how to use it.

When Alan and Agnes returned a few days later, a tall, distinguished looking man with thick white hair was with them. It was their friend Jack Summers, and he was walking without a limp.

He took hold of my hand and grinned. "I told Alan that I must come and thank you personally."

I invited them in and asked Kath to put the kettle on for tea.

"I was skeptical at first," Jack confessed as he settled in one of our few chairs.

"It was a little too unorthodox for him," Alan added with a smile.

Jack glanced at Alan and turned back to me. "When Alan gave me your handkerchief and explained what it was for, I thought he had gone daft. I didn't want to be unkind, so I took the handkerchief and thanked Alan for his concern. I remember thinking, 'How on earth can this possibly work?'"

Alan nodded his head with a look that said, 'I told you so.' Jack leaned forward and studied me for a few moments, as if I was possibly the most interesting person in the Universe. His eyes were bright, and I could feel his appreciation even when he wasn't speaking.

"Three days later, for the first time in five months, I was pain free! I can't thank you enough."

We became instant friends. I soon learned that Jack was an outstanding artist who had a painting exhibited at the Royal Academy of Art in London. Over the next two months I gave Jack four more additional treatments before he was free of all the effects of the crippling disease. On the last visit, I told him of Roche Bentley's offer, and that I didn't know where to start.

"I'll write it for you, Malc. I've written several books," he said grinning. "It will be my pleasure to do it for you."

Something this perfect had to come from heaven! The time between my decision to open our home again to the sick and needy after baby Katie, and Jack's appearance at my door, had been less than a month! I had been off the field for two years, but once I got back into the game, the Universe didn't waste a minute! It couldn't have worked better if I had planned it myself! In the space of a few weeks, I had an offer to publish a book, and now a published author to write it.

Over the next few weeks Jack and I spent many hours together during which I gave him as much information as I could recall about my life and the many healing "miracles" I had witnessed. It didn't take Jack long to complete what at times was a moving account of my healing work, and by the end of 1987, the book was ready to go to press. We decided to call the book *Healer!*, and 3,000 copies were printed in early 1988. It was a great feeling to see myself in print — a bit of an ego trip, I guess, but a pleasure nonetheless! I asked Roche to deduct the costs of publication from the book sales and to distribute whatever profits were left to a children's charity. Once again, I did not want to be making a profit out of the illness and suffering of others.

DISCOVERING EDGAR CAYCE

I started to see people on the last Sunday of the month. At the most, five or six people would come, but even with the memory of baby Katie behind me and having my book in print, I could not summon up the same enthusiasm that I had only a couple of years ago. The effects of debt and prolonged unemployment were taking their toll. I had lost confidence in myself, and not only that, I began believing I had lost any ability and skills that I had possessed before. I felt I had wasted my gift, that God had really intended it for someone else and I had gotten "the gift" by mistake, and now He had taken it back.

My interest in healing work was renewed, but my heart wasn't in it. Even when a lady who was totally blind began to get her sight back after a couple of visits, I was unmoved. It seemed nothing could rekindle the flame that once burned so fiercely within me. It felt strange, as if I had lost someone I loved with my whole heart, and realizing, now that she was gone, how much I truly yearned to be with her. I prayed to have that fire burning, to have that former passion return. Someone — a healing angel, or perhaps the mysterious, tall man with a beard — felt my yearning and my prayer was answered.

Two days before Christmas, along with a few Christmas cards, a small package arrived with a thud on the floor. The package was hand addressed, covered with USA stamps, and showed no return address on the outside.

"Who's sending me something from the USA?" I wondered.

In 1984, when the "Handkerchief Healer" story went out on the wire, a lady in El Paso, Texas, read about me in the National Enquirer and hired a detective to find me. As a result, I went to Texas to give healing to her baby daughter, who had become paralyzed from the neck down while in the care of a baby sitter six months earlier. I stayed in El Paso for a week, administering healing to the baby. There was some improvement, but not full recovery. In the course of that time I met several people, including doctors at the hospital, who were interested in and sympathetic to hands on healing. But that was four years ago, and I hadn't really been in touch with any of them since.

There was no name or return address or legible postmark on the outside, and nothing on the inside either, not a letter, a card or a note to indicate who sent it. To add to the mystery, the package bore my new address, 37 Mill Lane! I didn't have a clue who in America would know that I had moved just a few months back. Even to this day, I still don't know who sent it.

Inside the package was a paperback book, *There Is A River*, the true life story of Edgar Cayce by Tom Sugrue. Who in the world is Edgar Cayce? And why would some unknown person in America send me a book about him? There was an air of mystery about this, a feeling similar to when I found the silver hand in the grass by the construction site. There was something more than a book here, a sense of something of great significance, but I was not quite able to put what it was in focus, or to give it words. I immediately opened the book and began reading - and didn't stop until I reached the last page!

Edgar Cayce became an instant hero to me. I was awed by the accounts of Cayce's amazing psychic abilities and his great healing work. With each turn of the page, I could feel a quickening in my soul, and the more I read, the more answers I seemed to get about my own circumstances. I read the whole book cover to cover in one sitting.

Cayce's life wasn't easy. He pursued his gift and struggled and struggled. He had been ridiculed and misunderstood, he saw his business burn to the ground twice, went bankrupt, had a son die in childbirth and almost lost his wife from postpartum complications. He lost the dream of his life, his hospital, during the Great Depression. Yet thousands of people were helped through his awesome gift of clairvoyance. People were healed of diseases and ailments considered hopeless by the experts of the day, and even more, were shown a spiritual pathway that could transform their lives. There was definitely a great and timely message for me in the pages of this mysterious gift.

In the back of the book, there was a brief description about the Association for Research & Enlightenment, (A.R.E.) the organization founded by Edgar Cayce and still continuing with his work more than 50 years after his passing into Spirit. The blurb indicated that the A.R.E. depended upon donations to continue its work. I felt a strong urge to make a donation.

I was out of work and had no money to send, so I did as Edgar Cayce often advised, "Use that in hand." I phoned Roche Bentley in London, and asked him to ship a case of *Healer!* free of charge to the A.R.E. for their bookstore. I felt uplifted, knowing any money from the sales of these books would help promote the work of one of the greatest psychics who has ever lived.

Despite the chaos of my life, something surely is guiding me — but toward what? And where? A poltergeist had gotten me to the Spiritualist Church; a sunbeam directed me to Harry Edwards' *Spirit Healing* when I was ready to walk away from my healing work before I had really discovered it. A healing hand appeared in the grass, and now when I am low, discouraged and questioning God about this "gift" I had been given, *There Is A River* manifests.

A few weeks later, a letter arrived from the A.R.E. thanking me for my donation. As far as I was concerned, that was the end of the matter. I did what I could and added my little bit to help with the work. I didn't realize it at the time — and it would be years away before I understood it — but that anonymous gift of *There Is A River* was the first of many blessings that would come to me through the lives that Edgar Cayce touched. But for now, there was no prospect of work, and I was struggling to keep my home and family intact.

BACK TO WORK AT LAST

Christmas came and went, and 1989 slumped in with a very somber face. January remained gloomy, and suddenly without warning at all, February smiled. A job loomed on the horizon, and everything seemed a bit brighter. The Monckton Coke & Chemical Plant just two and a half miles from me announced a number of job vacancies. The coke from this factory is not Coca Cola or an illegal drug you buy on a street corner, but the fuel which people throughout England burn on their fires to heat up their homes. The odds of even getting an interview were slim. The chances of being hired were even slimmer. When I went to apply over 100 people had already taken application forms. But the hand of God was on my shoulder. I not only made it through the interview, I got the job! After two years out of work, I was off the dole and on a payroll. It felt great to be among the working class again!

My job at Monckton Coke & Chemical would last for the next 12 years. It was grueling work among rows of huge ovens that burn eighteen tons of coal at a time. The ovens remove all the gasses and fumes from the coal and reduce it smokeless. It is then pushed from the ovens into railway cars to be taken away and processed into bricks for fuel. All the workers had to wear thick wooden clogs to keep the heat from the floor from rising up through their bodies, and we all walked around like spacemen wearing helmets with little fans inside to combat the gasses and fumes. In the summer the temperatures in the plant reached 100 to 125 degrees. The wage that we were paid was hardly a living wage. We worked an eight-hour shift, but the money was not enough to live on, so almost everyone asked to work overtime or extra shifts, making it a 16-hour day.

The same month that I went to work at the plant, Kath was hired at a multinational bakery in the village. With Kath and I working, our lives gained more stability. I decided to open up my home again to people in need of healing. I was on a rotating three-shift system, one week working the day shift, the next week, afternoons, followed by the dreaded night shift, which I hated. It was hard going, and became even more of a problem when our daughter Adele gave birth to Jade, our first grandchild, in August of 1992. Adele's pregnancy was without complication, but shortly after Jade was born, we discovered the baby had major health problems, and at four months old he underwent heart surgery. For many months, Kath and I spent all our spare time with Adele and Jade, some twelve miles from our home.

SHOWN IN A COMA

With a shortage of available time, I limited myself to seeing people on the last Sunday of the month, and only those with serious health problems. One of these was a young man named Dean. Dean lived in a village ten miles from my home, and until he came to my door, we had never met, nor did he have any connection with Ryhill where I live.

Two years before we met, Dean was in a near fatal car crash. For weeks it was uncertain whether the lad would live or die, and for two months, he lay comatose. While in the coma, Dean had a vivid dream, or out-of-body experience. He called it a "psychic dream." In his dream, a man appears and tells Dean he has to take him somewhere. He and the guide leave the hospital and with great speed, travel over the countryside, arriving at a house situated in a long row of terraced homes. The house has a distinctive well-manicured lawn on both sides of the path leading to the door, and the walls of the house are covered with lush, green ivy. The door is open, but Dean is not able to see inside.

"There's a man inside who will help you recover much faster than you expect," his guide says turning toward him. "When you are well enough to travel, you must come and see him."

"How will I find him? Where does he live?" Dean responds. The guide gives him the necessary information, and with that, the dream ends.

Eventually, Dean came out of his coma. He was severely brain damaged, which caused physical disabilities. He had speech problems, his hands were curled claw-like up against his chest, and he had great difficulty walking, but he was no longer in danger of losing his life. He was discharged and was allowed to live with his parents.

One day his mother saw one of my cards advertising Spiritual Healing in the window of a shop in her village. I had placed it there several weeks before when visiting Adele. She called that evening and asked if she could bring her son over for treatment. The appointment was made for the following day.

When they arrived, they were speechless. They both recognized my house with its manicured lawn and ivy on the walls as the very house that Dean had seen two years before in his dream. Simultaneously, Dean and his mother recalled a long forgotten fragment of his dream — the answer to his question, where will I find him, the man who will help me?

"In the village called Ryhill," the guide answered. Now, as if planned from long ago, they were in Ryhill, standing on my doorstep.

As Dean and his mother recounted their incredible story, I was more shocked than they were. I could not believe such things were possible, except his mother verified everything! Dean had recounted all the details of his "psychic dream" to his mother a long time before. At the time, I had no explanation how a young man in a deep coma some two years previous could describe with photographic accuracy the outside of my home and its location. Now, after many experiences of my own and listening to other stories equally as incredible from people I have treated, my understanding has vastly improved concerning how our spiritual guides and teachers on the Other Side keep watch over us and work to make sure what needs to happen does, as unbelievable as some of it may seem.

Dean continued to make regular visits for healing. After each visit a noticeable improvement followed, sometimes within days after the session.

"What, if anything, has your accident taught you?" I asked him one day, anticipating something predictable, like 'Don't ride in fast cars.' Instead, he surprised me.

"Spirituality," he replied. "I know now I am much more than flesh and bones."

Often we only become aware of who we really are in the full spiritual sense in times of adversity. Or, in Dean's case, a near fatal accident — and a visit from a guide.

CHAPTER EIGHT

VIRGINIA BEACH CONNECTIONS

The early years of the 1990's passed quickly. I continued working the three-shift system at the coke plant and grabbing as much overtime as I could to help pay off debts from the construction business. Because of my schedule, the number of people coming for healing kept slowly dwindling. However, I began receiving requests for distant healing from people in Virginia who were reading *Healer!* One of these was a woman named Kathy Holder who lived in the Blue Ridge Mountains of Western Virginia. Kathy wrote asking for help for her asthma. Another woman, April Rain Brown, discovered my book in the A.R.E. Library. An avid student of all things metaphysical, April wrote just to say how much she enjoyed the book. After a few letters crossed the Atlantic, April asked if I would like to come to do some healing work in Virginia Beach. Does the Pope know Latin! Of course! I said, and arrangements were made for me to come over for ten days in September, 1996.

I invited Betty, my psychic cousin, to join me. Betty always dreamed of going to America, so I didn't have to ask twice. Kath was eager to come as well, but her father was in failing health, and she wanted to be close by in case he needed her. In the meantime, April was busy setting up a schedule. She made arrangements for me to speak and demonstrate at the Heritage Store, a big health food store and metaphysical center near the oceanfront in Virginia Beach. She also contacted a metaphysical church, the Virginia Beach Fellowship Center, and scheduled an engagement there. But the top of the bill for me was that I would be demonstrating my healing gift in the very shadow of Edgar Cayce at the A.R.E. Center!

About a week before we were due to fly out, I received a call from the church in Virginia Beach. The lady on the other end of the line introduced herself as the Director of the Fellowship Center and said she had a few questions for me. I detected a London accent, and I was right. Her name was Judith Van Cleave, and she had been living in America for several years.

"I need to know your fee," she said, "so I can put it in the flier announcing your visit."

"Nothing," I told her. "There's no charge."

"I think you must have misunderstood me. What are your fees for healing?" She seemed slightly confused.

"There's no fee. It's God's energy." I said. "I don't have a fee for my healing work in England and the rules will be the same in the USA."

"I appreciate where you're coming from," she answered, "but I'm afraid it doesn't work like that in the States."

Now it was my turn to be confused.

"Our church, like many other small venues that sponsor speakers and healers like yourself, depends upon income from the event to help support ourselves. We take a third of the income generated by our speakers. A third of nothing is nothing, and we cannot keep the doors open on an income of nothing. So, again, how much is your fee?" Her voice was kindly, patient — and firm.

I didn't know what to say. My mind went blank. In all my years with the Spiritualist Church, no one ever charged for healing and I had made that my practice too. The idea of a set fee for giving healing was simply too foreign to my thinking. But the lady on the other end of the line wanted an answer. My eyes fell on a brochure on the table by the phone. April Brown had sent it to me and it had been lying there for weeks. It was from the Heritage Store and contained a calendar of events and speakers. Nothing on their schedule had anything to do with Spiritual Healing, however the average fee for their various offerings seemed to be about $30.00.

"Would $30 be OK?" I asked sheepishly.

"If that's all you want, then I guess we'll go with it," she conceded. "It doesn't seem like much, especially for coming all this way." Then she said with a smile in her voice. "See you next week. Have a good flight."

On the night before our flight, Kathy Holder and Art Augsten, her fiancé, called with unexpected but welcome news. They had rented a private house for Betty and me. It was their gift to us. It was a generous offer, and we felt blessed, relieved and grateful. In truth, Betty and I were struggling to make ends meet and concerned with what a week's stay at a resort hotel would cost us.

WE ARRIVE

We arrived in Norfolk on a Monday at the tail end of a hurricane. A hot rain lashed the September evening as the plane touched down. Kathy and Art met us at the gate. The voices I had known over the phone now had faces. Kathy gave us a welcome hug, and then introduced me to her fiancé. As Art reached for my hand I had an instant feeling that I knew him, but couldn't remember from where. He felt like someone I might have worked with years before, or an old school chum, or a long lost relative, but I just couldn't bring when or where into focus. "Who are you?" I blurted out, and immediately felt awkward and self-conscious. Kathy had just introduced us! It was overwhelming, more like a reunion than first introductions.

April was waiting inside. She had a tummy bug and wasn't feeling well. As we headed for the luggage carousel, I spotted a small-framed lady with blonde hair cut short. I knew it was April even before we were introduced. I felt an instant bond with her. Reincarnation was still a new idea for me, and I wasn't sure where I stood on it. In the Spiritualist Church, we have evidence of life after death, but opinions vary whether we come back or not. Was I really meeting up with people I had known and worked with before? I knew Edgar Cayce struggled with the concept when it first came up in his work. I decided I would just remain open, and see what happens.

On our way to our lodgings we drove past the A.R.E. A virtual chill went down my spine at the sight of the old Cayce Hospital on top of the hill.

101

"That's where the administrative offices are now, but it was the first holistic hospital in America," April said.

I closed my eyes and tried to imagine what it must have been like to be there when Edgar was alive, getting a reading, coming to the hospital for treatment. What an awesome experience to have known him. It was awesome just to know about him!

The wearying effects of our long journey through many time zones and no sleep started to take its toll as we brought our luggage in from the car, said our good byes and unpacked. We took the following day off in order to recover from the jet lag. My first lecture and demonstration was scheduled for 8:00 p.m. on Wednesday at the Heritage Store. April picked us up at 7:00 and took us to the store. Art and Kathy arrived early, and at the appointed hour, 25 people had taken their seats for the demonstration.

"Not a lot of people, to say we've come all this way," I whispered to Betty.

"It'll get better," she assured me.

"What if they can't understand me because of my accent?"

"Well, at least it's not Cockney. You'd need an interpreter for sure."

I was as nervous as a turkey at Christmas. Negative thoughts filled my head. I had my talk outlined in my head. I would introduce myself and tell the story of the psychic lady who told me I had the gift, how Kath was healed, how the gift developed, and of the poltergeist who brought me to Spiritualism. The demonstrations at the conclusion of the talk were my biggest concern. No matter how successful a healer is there are always certain people who do not respond to the energy. What if the volunteers I choose for the healing demonstrations are some of them? If the first demonstration doesn't work, would I lose my confidence?

Betty was sympathetic.

"Try not to worry so much," she said.

"What if the demonstrations aren't successful?"

"You'll be all right, Malc, trust me."

I needn't have worried. I told my story and tried not to dwell on my misfortunes, but could feel my anger in my belly as I quickly passed over those dark days without an income and the ingratitude and abandonment of the people I had helped.

I managed to get some sympathy and a laugh when I told about the fundamentalist lady in my village who said I was doing Satan's work and promised to dance on my grave. "Fine," I answered as the old sea man I was, "I plan to be buried at sea."

I also added the story of the strange gentlemen who phoned me up and asked if he could come and talk to me about Spiritual Healing. He came smartly dressed, was well spoken and as he walked toward me with his brief case, I thought he was a doctor. Unfortunately, he turned out to be some kind of fanatic. He accused me of doing the devil's work by taking away pain and suffering. At this stage I'd been doing healing for seven or eight years, and nobody had told me I am doing the devil's work. At first I didn't know what to say. I had to ask him what he meant.

"You are taking all this pain and suffering off people," he answered with an accusation. "God has put this punishment on people, and you are doing the devil's work by taking it from them!" Next he showed me in the Old Testament the passage that says the sins of the fathers are visited on their children down to the seventh generation. My temper surged up to the boiling point.

"You mean God is putting pain and suffering on children and people for something their great great grandfather did, and taking away their pain and suffering is the devil's work?"

"I think you've grasped it," he said.

"I think it's time you ought to go," I answered and pointed to the door.

"You'll dance in hell for what you're doing," he spewed back at me. His words stuck in my heart like a thousand spears, and I felt a desperate need for some tender loving care from my wife. Kath was in the kitchen washing dishes.

"What's wrong with you? You look like you've seen a ghost!"

"A guy just told me I'm doing the devil's work and I'm going to dance in hell."

"Well let's hope you can dance better there than you do here," she answered. It was just what I needed to hear.

The audience was warm and receptive as I went to baby Katie's healing miracle, Roche Bentley's offer, the timely appearance of Jack Summers and the mysterious arrival of *There Is A River* and how it brought me to Virginia Beach. I recounted some of the dramatic healing miracles from my ministry, and ended by asking for volunteers and chose three from the audience. The demonstrations lasted five to seven minutes each and each person experienced the energy. One felt a tingling through her body and dramatically reduced pain. The second experienced heat and dizziness and gained movement in her frozen shoulder. The third volunteer, a young man with an asthma condition, said he felt a loosening sensation in his lungs and was now breathing with much less effort. Everything went well and no one left disappointed. When it was over, April reported that Tom Johnson, the owner of the Heritage Store, wanted me back the following day for private sessions.

VIRGINIA BEACH TIME

My next public demonstration was scheduled for 7:00 p.m. the following night at the Fellowship Center, about 30 blocks away from the Heritage Store at the other end of the Beach. I spent the day giving sessions at the Heritage. At 6:00 p.m., someone was supposed to pick me up and take me to the Fellowship Center. It was almost 7:00 and a driver had yet to appear. Eventually someone from the Heritage Store volunteered to drive Betty and I to the church. She told us she was new to Virginia Beach and wasn't sure where the Fellowship was. It was twenty past seven when our driver pulled up in front of an old white wooden church on a residential street.

We were late, late, late, but the church was dark and empty. Not a single light on in the building. I panicked as the driver pulled away.

"Betty, we've got the wrong church!"

Betty was unflustered. She calmly stepped around the corner and spied a small bungalow behind the church.

"Look, there's a small house in the back. Go ask for help."

My heart rose. Lights were shining through every window. It must be the caretaker's cottage, I thought and trotted down the gravel drive for the door. Just as I was about to announce myself with a knock, a terrific argument exploded in the house. Tactfully, I backed away and made a hasty retreat back to Betty.

"Try telephoning someone." Betty suggested next.

"Good idea. But there's no phone in sight, and who am I going to call? I don't have any phone numbers."

The clock kept ticking. We were now forty minutes late. My heart was racing, spurred by my frustration and despair, while Betty stood by, totally calm and relaxed. It was annoying. What did she know, that I didn't?

A few more minutes passed, then a car stopped in front of the church, and a bright-faced, attractive woman with long straight hair stepped out of the car.

"You must be Malcolm," she said, totally unruffled "I'm Judith." She was the lady in charge of the church.

"Thank God, I thought we were at the wrong church."

Judith smiled back. "Oh, this is the Beach. Things happen when they're supposed to, not when the clock says." In other words, no one bothers too much about being dead on time I thought!

As she ushered us in to the little church, a sense of normalcy soothed my troubled mind. Soon, the sanctuary was full and we had a very successful evening. After the meeting was over, Judith announced that I would be returning to give healing sessions for the next two days.

Early the next morning, I was up and ready. My first appointment was scheduled for 9:00. The house Kathy and Art rented for us was only a few minutes from the church. I assumed someone would pick us up at least ten or fifteen minutes before the first appointment. An hour ticked by and no sign of anyone.

"More of this Beach time," I snorted, complaining loudly to myself about unreliable people and lax schedules. I was forty minutes into my second hour of grumbling and waiting, when I suddenly realized the fault was mine! I had given Judith the wrong address! My panic attack was interrupted by a sharp rat ta tat tat on the front door. It was one of the women from the Fellowship Center.

"You gave us the wrong address, that's why we're late," she said with a laugh. "We called the Heritage and got the right address." She didn't seem the least bit irritated at all, but I was embarrassed, yet thankful we had been found.

SPIRIT EMBRACE

After my last session on Friday, April arrived to take me back to my apartment. I was feeling a little tired, and looking forward to a little relaxation as we pulled away from the church.

"Malcolm, there's some people who want to meet you," April said. She explained that she belonged to a spiritual development group based on psychic readings given by Edgar Cayce. "I've told them all about you. Would you mind giving a little talk on Spiritual Healing, followed with healing for those who request it?"

I agreed. We stopped to pick up Betty, but she had already been invited out to dinner, and declined. When we arrived at our destination, there must have been 35 to 40 people packed into the living room, waiting for us. Our hosts, Karl and Peggy Poland, met us at the door. They appeared to be in their seventies and were one of the nicest couples I have ever met.

After my impromptu talk, I offered to give healing to anyone who asked, and all but one accepted. Just about everyone I touched went into a very quick sleep-like state. If you have ever been to a healing service, or watched healers on TV, you've seen a phenomenon called Slaying of the Spirit. The healer reaches out and touches the person, and he or she falls backward. Usually an assistant is standing to catch the person so they don't fall to the floor or get hurt. In my sessions, the client is seated, and I sit on a chair behind them. When the client slumps backward, I support them with my shoulder for the duration of the healing session.

There are two schools of thought about why people go into this trance-like state. One says the person is in great need of relaxation. The few minutes they are in this altered state leaves them both physically and mentally refreshed. The other theory is that during this sleep state the healing guides draw out the spirit body from the physical one and perform a spirit operation, if required. When the spirit body goes back to the physical shell, the work that has been done on the spirit body is transferred back to the areas in the physical that need it. As unconventional and unbelievable as it sounds, there

MALCOLM SMITH with ROBERT KRAJENKE

is ample evidence from healers and clients alike to support this theory, including my first client of the night.

He was a big fellow, over 6' 3" tall, with a major health problem. This was his first experience with Spiritual Healing. I put my hands on his head, and within twenty seconds he entered into a deep sleep. After ten minutes I gently brought him back by lightly squeezing his shoulders and touching his forehead. When he woke up, he was very emotional. I asked him to describe his trance experience. Still sitting in the chair and glancing around at everyone in the room, he told how angels had come and informed him that they had to do some work on his spirit which would help him with his health problem!

The most memorable healing of the evening occurred with the next person. I had an overwhelming feeling that there was a doctor in the room who had problems with his eyes. It turned out an eye doctor was sitting less than four feet away.

"Do you have any health problems?" I asked.

"No, not at all. I feel fine," he answered, shaking his head. Despite this, I had a strong feeling he was in need of some kind of healing.

"Would you mind sitting on the stool here," I asked, gesturing to the healing seat in front of me. I had never seen this man before in my life. I didn't know anything about him except that he said he was an eye doctor. As soon as I touched him I had an inner knowing that he had just lost his wife. Now, I am not a psychic. I am a healer. For most of my work, I have no special feelings of energy flowing through me. In fact, I try to keep my mind off what I am doing, and let whatever is going to be done get done without interfering by asking Spirit questions, visualizing or projecting symbols. But, sometimes I do get information coming through, and I am always of two minds whether to pass it on or not. I never know how my client will react. In this doctor's case I was very reluctant. He appeared to be in his early forties and, as I often doubt the validity of this psychic information when it does come, I decided to keep my thoughts to myself.

If you have ever seen the movie "Ghosts," you'll no doubt remember the scene where Patrick Swayze, the "ghost," is able to convince Demi Moore, his wife, through Whoopi Goldberg, the medium, that he's really present. The deceased husband and the living wife communicate, dance and experience the love and intimacy they had with each other before he died.

"Have you just lost your wife through breast cancer?" The words came out of my mouth. It was as if someone was forcing me to speak. The doctor turned and looked at me astonished.

"Yes!" he answered in a quiet, subdued voice. "How did you know that?"

Before I could explain, more information began coming through.

"The day after she died you went into the bedroom and you pulled out a blue sweater from one of her drawers. You sat on the edge of the bed and put the sweater to your face and wept into it. As you wept, you called out her name loudly." Tears started to overflow in his eyes.

"How do you know all this?"

"Is everything I have just told you true?" I was almost as astonished as he was.

"Yes. Everything. But how do you know these things?"

I confessed that I wasn't sure myself how I knew.

"It could be your wife," I answered. "I'm not sure."

He turned back to the healing position, wiping a tear from his cheek. I placed my hands upon his head, and immediately he fell into a deep and restful slumber. After a comfortable period of about ten minutes, I gently brought him back.

"I've just been with my wife," he said in an awed tone of voice. He appeared somewhat confused and emotional. "Please can you allow me just a few more moments for us to be together? Just a few moments."

A deep silence settled over the room. The doctor was obviously engaged in some profound, internal experience. I could see wet cheeks and tears in the eyes of more than a few in the room.

Once again I placed my hands on his head, and in moments, he was in trance. After another ten minutes, I gently began to rouse him. This time as he returned to consciousness, he was more at peace. He said that he had been with his wife.

"I could see her and speak with her," he said. The words they shared were private and personal, also emotional. "And just as I was being brought back to my body, I was able to hug and kiss her."

Later, several members of the group asked what my thoughts on this "healing experience" were. Was he really with his wife? Was it a dream? An out-of- body experience? What does it matter? He gained peace of mind. That's what matters. It wasn't a physical healing, but a spiritual one. The primary objective of Spiritual Healing is to stir the soul, and his soul had been touched. That night he went home and slept soundly for the first time in a long time. The next morning, he called just to say thank you and to relay how grateful he was for an experience he would never forget.

Sometime after 2 a.m. I crawled into bed, thanking God for the blessings and for the weekend ahead with Art and Kathy at their home in the Blue Ridge Mountains.

THE BEATLES FAN

Art and Kathy had arranged for one of their friends, Gay Hunt, to drive Betty and I to their farm some seventy miles north in the Blue Ridge Mountains. The drive through the magnificent Shenandoah Valley lifted my spirit and renewed me physically and mentally. Eventually we arrived at Covesville, the home of Art and Kathy. We left the main highway and turned onto a dirt road that turned and twisted upwards as we bumped along. The overhanging branches of ancient trees created a canopy of outstanding beauty. Shafts of sunlight pierced through the multitude of variegated Fall leaves. It was a very sacred experience.

"No one need go to India or climb mountains in Tibet to experience God," I remarked to Gay. "You have it all in these mountains!" Gay agreed, and asked me about Stonehenge and Glastonbury, England's spiritual centers, as we drove for a few more miles.

"This is it," Gay said, and pointed towards a magnificent Dutch style house nestled against a backdrop of lush forest. Art and Kathy and a young man came out from the house to greet us. After a round of hugs, Art introduced me to his friend, Frank Zaffino. Frank stood no taller than 5'3" and reminded me very much of a miniature version of Sylvester Stallone as "Rocky." In fact, Frank was an accomplished boxer and weight lifter with a passion for acting — and the biggest Beatle fan I have ever met.

"Have you ever met them?" he asked with great interest. "Had I ever been to Liverpool? How many Beatle records did I have?" His Beatle questions were endless.

Suddenly I had the same experience I had with Art at the airport. The deja vu lasted a split second. It wasn't as intense as it was with Art, but strong enough to get my attention, and cause me to revisit the idea of rebirth and soul memory. I was 50 years old and never had any major psychic experiences, unless you include the poltergeist that I had in my home and one out-of-body experience. Now, in a space of a week, four people came into my life who I seemed to know from another time. I was more convinced that Edgar Cayce had it right. Reincarnation is a fact. The purpose of a soul for coming into this world again and again is for spiritual growth and education — with the main lesson being love and forgiveness. We can't absorb all the lessons in a single lifetime, so we continue to return until mastery is gained. Then it's perfectly feasible that we meet up with the same souls that we knew in previous lives. The Earth is a school, and our "class mates" return as family, friends or indeed, in our most difficult relationships. Some of our greatest teachers are the people who give us the hardest lessons. When we meet up with these old souls, deep down a memory is stirred, creating the deja vu effect. It makes sense. On the other hand, any good psychiatrist could offer a more feasible, down-to-earth explanation. Whatever the reason for these close encounters doesn't really matter. Our little soul group had a most enjoyable reunion that weekend, and our friendship continues to this day.

"See you in England, Frank," I shouted as he drove slowly down the winding dirt road to the main highway, waving and smiling to us from the cab of his pickup. That memory will stay with me always. Two weeks later Frank was killed in an automobile accident. Like everyone else who knew him, I was devastated. In the short time I spent with him, Frank expressed an earnest desire to help bring healing and comfort to people. In death, he achieved his wish. His organs were donated for transplant. No less than 200 people benefited from his gift.

He never made it to Liverpool, but when he arrived in heaven I'm sure he got to meet his all time great hero — John Lennon!

MY BIG NIGHT AT THE A.R.E.

Monday, September 16, 1996. The time had arrived for the most anticipated event of all — my healing demonstration in the very shadow of Edgar Cayce's workplace, the A.R.E. Library & Conference Center in Virginia Beach! For me, this was the reason for the whole trip. To put it mildly, I was awe struck.

The demonstration was scheduled for 7:00 p.m. Betty and I arrived an hour early. As we pulled into the parking lot, I was gripped with the same emotional response to the old hospital building as I had on the first day we drove past it.

We were greeted at the door of the Conference Center and treated to a guided tour by a resident volunteer. We went through the lobby to an elevator and rode it to the second floor.

"This is the biggest metaphysical library in America," our volunteer announced as we stepped from the elevator into a large room with islands of small reading tables occupied by a mixed lot of people of various ages, nationalities and backgrounds, all doing research it seemed.

"You'll find information on any topic related to man's soul, health or search for God, including extremely rare and hard to find books on obscure and arcane subjects. That's why researchers from all over the world come here."

I was impressed. A library of sacred sciences. I remembered reading something about the great Library of Alexandria in Egypt. It was said to house all the knowledge of the world. Perhaps this is a taste of what it was like.

"And over there," our guide continued, indicating a corner of the library with shelves filled with thick, hardcover binders, "are the actual transcripts of all the Edgar Cayce readings, over 14,500 of them." My heart beat a little faster. I felt like a pilgrim in an ancient Hall of Records. An almost palpable energy seemed to fill that part of the room. In those files lay the great legacy of Edgar Cayce, a whole life's work of one of the most remarkable men in history — the "father of holistic medicine" — and a spiritual giant.

We lingered in the library for a few minutes, and then our guide escorted us to the meditation room on the upper floor for a few moments of silence, and back to the main floor and into a spacious auditorium. I gasped. Several hundred people could easily fit in.

"Betty I can't believe that I'm to do healing in this place. Look at the size of it!"

"Oh, you aren't healing in here," my guide interrupted. "This auditorium is for special occasions. You'll be in the mini. I'll show you."

She led us out of the auditorium and into a room that indeed was much, much smaller, perhaps with a capacity of 75. In truth, I was disappointed. My balloon had burst. What did she mean, "...for special occasions only?" In my mind, demonstrating God's healing power is always a special occasion. I was convinced that Edgar Cayce would consider channeling spiritual energy to heal the ills of body, mind and soul worthy enough for this wonderful auditorium. Suddenly, without a doubt, I knew I was destined to speak and work in this hall.

"Bett, one day I'm going to come back and do my healing here."

"I believe you will Malc," she replied with a knowing smile.

Then, 7:00 p.m. arrived and in no time at all the mini-auditorium was totally full. Soon it was standing room only, and people were being turned away. There was no room to place them. It was a very memorable night. People came forward with all types of illness - migraines, asthma, fibromyalgia, and cancer - to receive God's healing power. The demonstrations were no longer than five to seven minutes, and just about everyone who came forward testified to some kind of improvement. I worked on all that I could until the custodian came in and told us we were long past the normal closing time. The time had raced by, and the memory still remains strong in my mind. It was an experience I will cherish for as long as I live.

Before I knew it, we were back at Norfolk International where ten days before Art, Kathy and April met us with open arms and smiling faces. Now it was just Art and Kathy. April had to work.

I couldn't believe it. Our trip was finished. But it wasn't over by any means. Something new had just begun, and there was more to come.

We laughed, hugged, expressed our thanks and promised to stay in touch, a promise we all have kept to this very day. Then it was time to board the plane — and home again to England.

MIRACLE WITHIN A MIRACLE

Back home, I was asked a number of times if I had any outstanding stories of miracles I could share. There were many, but my favorite one — and one which I tell in my public lectures to this day — was given to me by a school teacher from Texas who received her miracle some twelve months before. I can't recall her name, but as she took her place on the stool in front of me, I guessed her age to be about 40. She was tall, slim and attractive with an air of great compassion about her.

"What's your problem?" I asked. She replied that she was having trouble sleeping and problems with her nerves. Guessing her condition was stress related, I asked what kind of work she did.

"I teach school."

"Trying to teach those young kids is pretty tough, I guess."

"No, just one of them."

"And what was his problem?" I asked, being a bit nosey.

The lady didn't respond. The silence extended for a few moments. I felt I had to wait until she was ready to speak. Finally she understood I wasn't going to give up, and she began her incredible story.

"I was a tenth grade school teacher teaching mostly 15 year olds, in a small town close to the Texas/Mexican border. One of my new students was a boy from a Mexican family that was 'the poorest of the poor.' They had just moved to the area. On the first day of school, the boy didn't even have a coat."

Out of compassion for the boy, she took him to a local dry goods store and bought him a new coat with her own money.

"Things seemed fine for a while," she said, biting her lip, "and then the boy started playing hooky. As his teacher, I was obligated to report his absences to the school principle." She sighed, coughed quietly and continued slowly. "A few days later at first bell, as the kids were filing into the classroom, the boy walked in, wearing his new jacket. He screamed at me, 'I thought you were my friend, bitch!'" Her voice trembled. By now I knew her experience had been extremely traumatic, and I felt a tinge of guilt for pressing her to reveal it.

"He started undoing the buttons as he came at me. When he got to the last button, the coat opened. I saw a handgun stuffed into his trouser belt. In that instant I knew he had no intention of harming the children. He was coming for me." She stopped and took a deep breath. I wished I hadn't been so nosey. She exhaled and with a struggle continued.

"The door was still open, and I rushed toward it. I had to go past him to get out. He jerked out the revolver and fired, almost at point blank range. The bullet grazed my forehead and knocked me down so hard that I broke both my arms. He walked over to me. I was crying and confused and struggling to sit up. He bent down, never saying a word, and put the gun to my temple and squeezed the trigger. Nothing happened, the bullet jammed. He tried to fire again, and the gun jammed again. He stayed as cold as ice. No emotion. Nothing. He just snapped the gun open, removed the bullets from the chamber, dropped them in one pocket and pulled more from another and reloaded. He snapped the gun back, put the barrel to my head, and pulled the trigger. Again, nothing happened - the bullet jammed yet again. The boy shook his head - he couldn't believe it. He just walked away, the gun still in his hand."

At this point she began to sob, obviously back in the nightmare, reliving all the emotions. I passed her a Kleenex to wipe her tears away. After regaining her composure she flashed a tentative, but brave smile at me.

"Can I ask you a question, Mr. Smith?"

"Ask away."

"Do you think, perhaps, that I had a guardian angel with me that morning?"

"No, I don't." I reached for her hand. "I think we must be talking four or five, at least!"

"I guess so." A trace of the smile remained on her lips.

Every now and then I'll get asked a question, something like this - "Does God work His miracles only through healers?" The answer, of course, is NO. NO, a thousand times NO. Miracles happen every day to saints and sinners alike. It doesn't matter who you are, where you are, how old you are. We are all here for a purpose, and the only ones who can get in the way of that are us. You can have your head and shoulders in the "Jaws of Death" just as this lady, but if it's not your time to leave the body behind, there will be a spiritual intervention.

"Just out of interest," I asked, "what happened to the boy? Is he in some kind of prison or detention center?" I just wasn't prepared for how fast we could go from the miraculous to the incredulous.

"You aren't going to believe this," she said, her voice filling with anger. "They have this irrational, unbelievable law in Texas. If a minor shoots you and the bullet doesn't pass through a vital organ, they don't have to go to a court of any kind. The following week the boy was back in my classroom, in the same school. I knew for a fact that once my arms healed and I was back teaching he would come for me again. So I quit my job and put as many miles as I needed between him and me - and that's how I came to be here in Virginia Beach. I have friends here."

As I listened to this young schoolteacher, I didn't doubt that her life was spared, because God has a plan for her, otherwise she wouldn't still be here. Perhaps part of that plan was getting her out of that little border town in Texas on a spiritual journey to Virginia Beach, where new possibilities and relationships exist for her. I thought back to the poltergeists in my own home. I feared the ridicule of the miners in my village if they discovered I was doing something as strange and bizarre as putting my hands on people and declaring myself a healer. The poltergeist drove me out of the house to the Spiritualist Church at Elmsall, and there I found my answer. Through the Spiritualist Movement my healing gift was nurtured and I found Tommy Smith and Harry Edwards. That was what I needed to keep developing my healing ministry.

A gun that jams three times is no accident. If we could but see it from the highest perspective, we would know everything occurs in Divine order for the highest good, and very little happens by chance.

Miracles happen, and when they do, sometimes they carry other miracles inside them. There is something very marvelous about Virginia Beach. In one of his Readings, Edgar Cayce described it as "a port for the White Brotherhood," indeed a very high spiritual center. And many a soul, tossed and churned on life's stormy seas, has found a refuge and safe harbor here. Perhaps, coming to Virginia Beach helped this lady move forward in her life. I never saw her again, and probably will never know what happened to her, but in my book, her story tops the list of "that's incredible."

I am sure the angels are still watching over her to this day.

A LIFE SAVED

I had only been home a couple of days and still on a high from my trip to America when the doorbell rang. It was my cousin Joan.

"What brings you here so early on a Sunday morning?"

Joan slumped into a chair and began weeping uncontrollably. "What's wrong Joan?" I asked anxiously as I placed my arm around her to comfort her.

Joan is a first cousin, but she has been as close as a sister to me. She is one of ten children who were raised in a tiny "two up two down" row house with no electricity and no bathroom. If you needed the toilet, it was fifty yards from the house and shared by your next-door neighbors. Yet the love in that house was awesome. I spent more time at Joan's house than mine. My wife Kath and Joan have always been close. In fact it was Joan who introduced me to Kath. It's said that an only child is a lonely child - but not when you're raised and loved by an army of cousins!

Joan struggled with her grief and between her sobs managed to choke out her story.

"Chelsea is dying," she moaned.

Chelsea, her teenage daughter, had a history of drug addiction. She had been through several court ordered drug abuse programs. But within days of being released, after weeks of treatment, she'd be running with the same crowd and her drug use continued.

"Are you sure she's dying?" I asked.

Tears rolled down her eyes as she poured out the details.

"A few days ago, Chelsea became seriously ill. She grew worse by the hour, and we rushed her to the hospital. The tests showed all of her main organs are damaged beyond repair. Her kidneys and liver are malfunctioning and she has Hepatitis C." Joan fumbled in her purse for a tissue. I handed her one from the table next to me, and she wiped her eyes. "Her whole body is shutting down, Malc."

Twelve months earlier, Chelsea had given birth to a beautiful baby boy. Because of Chelsea's drug problem, Social Services placed the baby in Foster Care until Chelsea could stay drug free and healthy enough to have him back. The tragedy Joan faced now was not only losing her only daughter, but her only grandson as well. My heart ached for her.

Joan looked up with all her grief and pain reflected in her eyes. "We brought her home to die, Malc. After we got her settled in, she took a critical turn, and we sent for our family doctor. When he finished examining her, he came out of her room and started to cry. 'Give her all the love and comfort you can,' he said. 'She's fading fast. She won't last the day.'"

Long after the doctor left, Joan and her husband Jack remained numb with shock, unable to comprehend that soon their precious daughter would be no more. Suddenly, the brutal finality of her daughter's eminent death jolted Joan from her trance. She grabbed her coat and rushed for the door.

"Where are you going?" Jack cried out.

"To see our Malc. Maybe he can help her."

And that's how it came to be that on a foggy Sunday morning I was standing at Chelsea's bedside as the court of last resort. Chelsea was as gaunt as a skeleton. Her skin was yellow and she kept drifting in and out of consciousness. I had known her since she was a baby, yet I could hardly recognize her.

"Why are the curtains drawn?" I whispered to Joan.

"Chelsea can't tolerate any light, daylight or electric," she answered.

I leaned close to Chelsea. "Chelsea, do you remember who I am?"

"Uncle Malc," she replied weakly. "I'm so cold, Uncle Malc. I'm so cold."

I knelt by the side of the bed, and for the next half hour, moved my hands over the major centers and plexuses of her body as Joan stood by and watched.

"May God have mercy on my beautiful niece," I prayed as the energy passed through me into her. When I finished, I asked her how she felt. She managed a faint smile.

"Great, I feel lovely and warm. Will you come and see me again, Uncle Malc?"

Tears ran down my cheek as I bent over and kissed her gently on her forehead. I brushed my tears back hoping, in this dimly lit room, Joan or Chelsea could not see them. In my heart, I believed the next time I saw Chelsea she would be dead.

That evening I returned with my wife Kathleen. As we stood outside the house I reminded Kath that she had to remain strong.

"If you get too emotional," I warned her, "it'll make it harder for Joan and Jack. They are already on emotional overload."

I opened the back door and we entered the kitchen and walked into the living room. Chelsea was sitting in front of the TV eating a meal! I was stunned.

Kath turned to me with a puzzled look.

"I thought you said she was dying," she whispered. I had no reply. Then Joan caught sight of us, her face lit with a gleeful smile and she rushed toward us.

"I don't know what you did, Malc, but whatever it was, it worked." She turned and pointed to Chelsea. "Can you believe it — that's the third meal she's eaten since you left her this morning!"

Her jaundice had gone. She was without pain, and she had the strength and appetite of a normal teenager. It didn't seem possible that only nine hours before I was convinced I would never see her alive again.

The miracle continued. With each passing day she grew stronger. Her major organs continued functioning normally. Even her hepatitis cleared up. Then the best day of all - her son was given back to her.

Two years have passed, and Chelsea continues to do well. To my best knowledge, she remains drug free. I am still awed by the speed of her recovery. It truly was a miracle. I am continually amazed and puzzled by the way this healing energy manifests. Some people who are more dead than alive receive a major miracle, while others with minor problems that seem easily curable often receive nothing at all. It's all a mystery. But, as I said before, the Jaws of Death can have you by the head and shoulders but if it isn't your time to die, then the Guy Upstairs will come to the rescue.

PROPHECY FULFILLED

"You're looking a bit down in the dumps," cousin Betty said as she greeted me at the door. On an impulse, I had decided to visit her. It had been almost three weeks since our trip to Virginia Beach, and I was feeling a bit down after the great high of that experience.

"Well, to be truthful Bett, I miss doing my healing work in America."

"Have you heard anything from anyone since you've been back?"

"Only from Art and Kathy."

Betty poured me a cup of tea.

"Would you like a reading Malc?" She pushed the cup toward me.

"Well, to be truthful, that's the reason I'm here."

I have great respect for Betty's clairvoyance. Even the police come to her for help on difficult cases. She doesn't need to read cards or use devices to tune in. She gets it direct for the asking. My reading lasted less than twenty minutes.

"You'll be asked to go back to work in Virginia Beach in November," she announced.

"Are you sure?" I could feel the blues lift from my shoulders.

"I'm positive."

September passed. October came and November dragged on. Each day I waited for the postman, but nothing came from the States. Days of disappointment turned into weeks. Still no invitation. With only four days left in November, I was deeply disheartened and desperate. I decided to pay Betty another visit and tell her, for once, she had got it dead wrong.

We exchanged greetings, and she took my jacket to hang up.

"I thought you said I would be going back to America in November, Bett. Well, November's over and I'm still here."

119

"No, Malc, you've got it wrong." Her voice was loving but firm. "I said that you would be asked to go back to work there in November. I didn't mean you would actually go there physically."

"I don't care what you say you meant. You got it wrong, this time."

Why wouldn't she just admit it? No one — not even a psychic — is a hundred percent right all the time. Edgar Cayce didn't always have it right, either!

I left Betty on a wave of discouragement. My trip to Virginia had left me with a profound feeling that I was destined to do my healing work in America. I never doubted I'd go back, and Betty had confirmed it. Now my faith was shaken. As November drew to a close, whatever ray of hope remained was dim indeed. My doubts grew, and their shadows were long. I feared my future in America was not to be.

On November 30, the last day of the month, a letter arrived from the Heritage Store. Inside was an invitation to come over and a contract to sign! Betty had it right! It was a miracle! My spirits soared. I could have danced all night!

The contract called for me to work ten days and return every four weeks, beginning in mid-January, 1997. Tuesday through Saturday I would work from 9 a.m. to 9 p.m. with breaks in between for lunch and dinner, Sundays would be afternoon only, and Monday was my free day. And the odd part — or the God part — was that what the Heritage proposed fit perfectly with conditions at Monckton Coke & Chemical. We were on a new work schedule of 12-hour days for 28 days straight, followed by eleven days off for rest and recovery. It was a perfect fit.

The Heritage Store is only one block from the ocean, but I saw very little of the beach. My schedule stayed full, and on Sunday mornings, I would meet with Art, Kathy and Gay for breakfast. My least favorite day of the week was Monday, my full day off. I wasn't brave enough to drive in America, and you need a car to get anywhere because of the distances. I resigned myself to spending the day reading or watching TV.

At the Heritage Store, some tension developed between the people in charge and me. When I began working for them, I explained that no one would be turned away who couldn't afford to pay. There would be no charge for children, people with terminal cancer or those who were out of work. The store did have a "tithing" policy, they explained — 10% of the scheduled sessions could be charity cases. Otherwise people who wanted a session had to pay, regardless. I agreed reluctantly, but remained angry and annoyed at their restrictions. After my own troubles, losing my house and being unemployed, my heart went out to the hardship cases. I could have filled up the day with them. I saw the Heritage's point clearly enough, and on many occasions I did manage to partially overcome the problem by taking the difference out of my pocket for those who didn't have enough money to cover the cost of the healing session.

Because of our differences and the limitations placed on me, the situation was not as pleasant as I would have liked it to be. But my conviction was stronger than ever that my healing ministry was to be in America. So, despite their policy, I could always find my way back to a feeling of gratitude and appreciation for the opportunity the Heritage Store provided. It was less than perfect, but it still felt like God's hand was in it. After the original three-month contract at the Heritage Store expired, we continued with the same ten-day, four-week arrangement but without a signed agreement.

ON TO CHICAGO

All through the months, I knew I would speak again for the A.R.E. and when the invitation came, it didn't come from Virginia Beach — but from A.R.E. enthusiasts in Chicago!

One night, when I was back home at the end of my shift at the plant, Kath called me to the phone. "It's long distance, from America," she said handing me the phone. The lady on the other end of the line introduced herself.

"My name is Diane Haggerstrom and I am an A.R.E. member in Chicago. We'd like to have you come here to speak."

Diane discovered my book *Healer* in the A.R.E. bookstore while at a conference in Virginia Beach. She took it home and was so impressed by what she had read that she began besieging her local A.R.E. coordinator, Toni Romano, to invite me to speak at the Chicago Center. Toni was reluctant, but agreed to give it a try.

My first visit to Chicago was in May 1997. Toni made up a flyer and promoted my talk in her newsletter. The night of the talk, the room was full and everything went extremely well. People laughed at my jokes, they seemed to understand me despite my accent, and the three volunteers I chose for the healing demonstrations all felt the energy and showed improvement. I was able to lengthen a shortened leg, give relief to an elderly lady with stiff arthritic joints, and provide a jolt of energy to a young woman suffering with chronic fatigue. For the next three days, the schedule was full with people coming for healing.

I was very comfortable with the people in Chicago, and they seemed impressed by what they saw. Toni and her staff of volunteers were really interested in what I was doing and saw it in terms of a spiritual mission without the financial or business concerns that I experienced at the Heritage Store. At last, I was working among kindred souls, truly spiritual souls who gave their love and time serving God without the need for anything in return. I felt, as I had with Art and Kathy, April and Frank, stirrings of memories, as if these were people — long, lost, loving family members — whom I had known before!

"Oh, we probably knew each other in Egypt with Ra Ta," Toni said, referring to one of the past lives of Edgar Cayce. The Cayce readings say that anyone who is drawn into the work of the A.R.E. has a past life connection with Cayce from the time of Ra Ta in ancient Egypt. "You were probably a healer back then," Toni added with a smile.

Chicago now was added to my schedule. I worked the demanding 12-hour/28-day cycle at the foundry, followed by five days at the Heritage Store and five days for the A.R.E. in Chicago, then back to England again to family and foundry. It was a grueling schedule, but it was God's work — and at the end of the day, I always felt richly blessed by the energy and the people I was privileged to serve.

CONGRESS WEEK

After my first visit to Chicago, the following month I was back at the Heritage Store when I received an invitation to speak at the A.R.E. during Congress week. It's peculiar, looking back now, that I don't recall who it was that invited me to speak to the Congress. Perhaps, I mused, it was the same anonymous soul who sent me that copy of *There Is A River* that started all of this. Regardless, my intuition about speaking in the main auditorium at the A.R.E. was about to be fulfilled.

Through my growing number of A.R.E. friends in Virginia Beach and Chicago, I was learning more about the A.R.E. — its study group program, conferences, workshop and field services. For the truly dedicated, the main event of the year is the Congress, always held in June. Delegates from Search For God groups from all over the U.S. and Canada — and even from overseas — come to work together, interact with staff, form plans and strategies, and air complaints to the headquarters staff. It is a very high energy, intense week with very motivated people.

I was asked to speak on Monday, the first day of Congress. That was wonderful. Monday was my day off from the Heritage Store, and I readily agreed. When I arrived at the Conference Center, one of the members, Patrick Walch, met with me and explained the evening was on a strict timetable. My "spot" was to be no more than one hour because another speaker would follow me. He also explained other speakers would be making presentations at the same time in other parts of the building. In the auditorium, the chairs were stacked and pushed along the walls creating a giant clear space.

"How many chairs should we set up?" I asked. "About thirty seems right, don't you think?"

Assuming each of the speakers would attract a small percentage of the anticipated audience, Patrick and I set out 30 chairs in three rows of ten. The chairs seemed minuscule in relation to the empty room.

"Oh well," I thought as I surveyed the hall from the stage, "at least I can say I worked in the main auditorium. Anything over 30 people would induce stage fright straight away!"

The doors opened early and people began wandering in. The 30 seats were quickly taken, and Patrick and I began hurriedly setting up more chairs, which were quickly filled. Soon, we used up all the stacked chairs along the walls, and began bringing more in from other rooms. By 7:00 p.m. the auditorium was at full capacity. It was standing room only and time to begin!

My friend Toni Romano stepped up to the platform to introduce me. My heart was racing and my fingertips felt ice cold. Someone clipped a microphone to my shirt. I took a deep breath to calm myself, and then another.

"Please give a warm welcome to Malcolm Smith," Toni said, gesturing toward me. I felt physically sick. I stood up. The audience responded with loud applause. My legs grew wobbly as I made my way up to the stage and reached out and hugged Toni. "Good God," I prayed desperately, "give me some of her strength for the next 60 minutes."

Toni stepped from the stage and took her seat in the front row. I looked down at her.

"Toni, have you got any Valium in your handbag?" I blurted out.

The audience roared with laughter, and my stress level dropped fifty degrees. However, my legs still felt weak, so I did most of my lecture sitting down. When it came time for the healing demonstration, three individuals, each with a different health challenge, came forward. In a short time, they all received visual, marked improvement. Then it was over. My hour was up. I felt at the pinnacle of my career as a healer. To do healing anywhere is an honor, but to do it in the shadow of Edgar Cayce on the grounds he had dedicated for his healing work, in the library that contained all the information he channeled, among people who were dedicated to his work — was an experience hard to put into words. I knew then what I had felt for so long was true — my work would be in the States, and all these people somehow would be part of it.

As I stepped from the stage, A.R.E. coordinators, including one from Germany, pressed around me with invitations of work. The first to reach me was Sylvia Chappell, the Events Coordinator for the A.R.E. of New York Center. I promised Sylvia that as soon as circumstances would allow, I would contact her with regard to visiting the A.R.E. Center in New York. Not being able to accept all these offers was like watching a great celebration through a window. People were inviting me in — but the door was locked, and I couldn't open it. But I felt that if God wanted me to do this work, a way would be found.

My desire to heal was a virtual compulsion. It is something I knew would never go away. Healing work was something I had to do, wanted to do, must do ... and I had a strong inner conviction that it would be in America.

A whole year passed before my financial situation in England improved to such an extent that I was able to keep my promise to Sylvia. I parted company with the Heritage Store and added New York to the schedule. My time away from Monckton Coke & Chemical was now divided between New York and Chicago. It was a demanding, yet satisfying schedule.

CHAPTER NINE

MY CONTRACT WITH GOD

Spiritually, I knew I would never be satisfied until I could devote all my time to healing. At the human level, I didn't know how long I could physically endure working the grueling 12-hour/28-day cycle at the plant, broken by ten, 12-hour days doing healing work in the States, and hours of sleepless travel back and forth over the Atlantic. My experience at Congress presented tantalizing possibilities of going full-time again into healing work, yet any thought of putting my family at risk was sobering. To give in to the urge — however divine its source — was to risk another disaster.

Once you try to achieve some great purpose in your life, and you fail, the first time down is a long, terrifying journey tumbling through a bottomless pit that keeps you wondering if you ever can climb out. But once you've been through it, you know what to expect if there's a second time down that awful road. You know because you've been there. Bad times don't go on forever; there's always an end to them. You pray that you'll never have to bottom out again, but if you do, you know you can move forward. It's never the end.

My desire to give healing was a compulsion that simply could not be wished or willed away. If it had just been me, I was willing to risk it all and give over to this urge completely, but I had a moral obligation to put Kath and our home above my needs. The kids were grown. Adele was out of the house with her own family. And there were still the debts owed, the mortgage and bills to pay. I struggled with these two minds, and the inner conflicts at times could exhaust and depress me, make me irritable and angry — or force me to become stronger and more resolved.

I decided to settle it once and for all. If this urge to heal was coming from God, and it was meant for me to surrender to it completely, then God would have to make it crystal clear with no possibility of mistake or misinterpretation. To make it even more bulletproof and ironclad, I put it to God this way: "God, let's make a contract, just like in the Bible. I will do what you want without any questions. If you want me to work at the plant, I'll do it until I die or you show me otherwise. If you want me to go out and heal the sick, because the need is great, then you'll have to show me with a sign."

I knew in my heart what that sign would be. It wouldn't be a burning bush or a parting of the waters, and when it showed up, I would know for certain I could no longer serve two masters — God and Monckton Coke & Chemical. I would be His, 100%.

THE SIGN

I always loved the album *Canadian Pacific,* by Country & Western singer George Harrison IV. The music was something, right from the very beginning, that I associated with my healing work. On that very first night when I drove with my copy of *Spirit Healing* to see Maralyn Mount, the songs from *Canadian Pacific* eased my fears and brought me comfort. I played it over and over again that night, and all through the early years it was my album of choice on my way to do my healing visits. The music never failed to soothe and relax me. Somewhere along the way, I don't recall how, I lost the cassette and was never able to replace it. I looked for it everywhere I could in England. Nobody ever seemed to have heard of it. Even with help from my A.R.E. friends, no copy could be found in Virginia Beach, Chicago or New York. I was told it was unavailable and out of print.

When I made my contract with God, I knew *Canadian Pacific* was the sign God would send. When that album was back in my hands, I would know it was time to return to a full-time healing ministry, no questions asked.

In my mind, it was an unalterable contract.

BETTY'S NEXT PROPHECY

Another year went by working with the A.R.E. Centers in Chicago and New York. In the early part of 1999, The Fellowship Church in Virginia Beach invited me back. This was exciting news. I missed Virginia Beach, especially Art, Kathy and April. Straight away, I telephoned cousin Betty.

"Betty, I've been invited back to Virginia Beach," I shouted into the phone.

"Well," she said nonplused, "you'll only go three times. You'll not go back any more than that."

What! I couldn't believe my ears. I had been going to Chicago for almost two years now, and New York for almost a year — and my schedule was full. Why wouldn't it be the same in Virginia Beach, a spiritual mecca?

"No way, Betty. You've got it wrong this time."

"You are going for a door to be opened for you." Betty replied, ignoring my comment. "You won't be going back."

I couldn't wait to prove her wrong.

When I arrived in Virginia Beach, I was certain Betty was off the mark. The church couldn't accommodate all the requests for healing. Every available appointment was taken. Indeed, people were on a waiting list. Sorry, Betty, but you're wrong.

On my second visit a month later, the first cracks in the wall appeared. The appointments slipped from 60 to 18. Quite a drop! Judith was gone, and there was a new director at the church, who offered a host of reasons for the poor turn out. She was new on the job. The newsletter wasn't mailed on time. She thought somebody else was handling the scheduling. People didn't know I was here. She apologized and assured me on my next visit, things would be different.

She was right.

It was worse.

When I arrived, it looked promising. There were cars parked in front of the church, and people were waiting inside to be seen. The trouble was they weren't waiting for me. The church had scheduled another healer, a psychic chiropractor from Louisiana, who was already busy in the healing room with a client. The church had double booked us for the same dates! During my seven days there, I saw no more than six people. It was just as Betty had predicted — a dead end. I wouldn't be coming back. But that was only one part of her prediction. She also saw a door opening for me. As far as I could tell, there was no evidence of anything opening for me, only shutting down.

On my last break on the seventh day, the receptionist handed me a piece of paper with a phone number and name written on the slip.

"Someone called from Detroit wanting to talk to you."

I took the note, put it in my shirt pocket, and went back to the healing room. My last client was waiting, and the note went quickly out of my mind. I didn't see it again until I was back home in England. I decided I would call the number in a month from New York.

CONNECTING WITH DETROIT

Sometimes - not too often, but occasionally - I get profound statements coming from people when they sit in front of me. My favorites are from the kids. I was back at the A.R.E Center in New York on my next visit to the States, and a lady brought her son to me. He was seven-years-old with no major health problems.

"He's very hyperactive," his mother explained.

I sat the boy on the stool, and as I looked him over, I thought how do I explain what I do to a seven-year-old child. As I'm having this thought, the boy says, "So what do you do?" Is this kid psychic or what!

"I've got magic hands," I answer. "I put my hands on people and that makes them big and strong."

"That's great," he replies and points toward my table. "What's that on the table?"

"Relaxation tapes."

"Do you have any classical music?"

"You like classical music?"

"I play the violin."

His mother sat on a chair about two feet away. I put one of the tapes in the cassette player, and put my hands on his head. In the space of a couple of minutes his head fell to his chest and he went into the relaxation mode. Without looking up, he says to his mother, "I do believe the power of God is flowing through me."

His mother put her hand to her mouth and looked at me stunned.

"Say that again, son."

"I do believe the power of God is flowing through me," he says again, word for word.

"Where did he get a statement like that?" I asked his mother when the session was over.

"I haven't a clue?"

"Do you go to church regularly?"

"We're good people, but we don't go to church regularly."

"How often is he hyperactive?"

"Only on weekends, when he doesn't have his music lesson."

"Well, let him be hyperactive on the weekend," I offered. "I think you've got a genius there."

That seemed to satisfy the mother, and she left pleased. On my next visit to New York eight weeks later, I saw them again, and the mother reported her boy was doing laying on of hands on family members and their pets.

When I had my next break that day, I made my call to Detroit. A man answered, and I introduced myself.

"Malcolm Smith! Oh my, that was well over a couple of months ago. I had just about given up hearing from you." The voice on the other end of the line belonged to Robert Krajenke, an A.R.E. author who had written four books on the Edgar Cayce readings and the Bible. "We read about you in the Fellowship Newsletter. I used to be the Director there a few years back."

Hmm, I wondered, was he as effective as the other director?

Robert explained that his wife, Lynne, had urged him to invite me to Michigan after reading about me in the Fellowship Newsletter. She had some potentially serious health challenges, and she was concerned about her mother who had a degenerative eye problem. And there were grandkids, too, Robert added, who could use my help.

"With the A.R.E. community here, the Unity Churches and our own family, I think we've got enough here to keep you busy."

"I can come in October." I answered. Detroit is only 200 miles from Chicago, so it seemed easy enough to split some time with Chicago. This had to be the door that Betty saw. There was nothing else that had come from that last trip to Virginia Beach. But where would it lead? I wanted to know.

UNMISTAKABLE AND CLEAR

I went straight from my job at the plant to pick up my bags at home. The taxi ride from Ryhill to the airport in Manchester took over an hour and a half. The flight across the Atlantic added another restless seven hours with no sleep, plus another hour or two going through customs in New York, and more waiting for my connecting flight to Detroit. When my plane touched down at Detroit's Metro airport, I was dog tired and looking forward to a cup of tea and a warm bed.

Robert was waiting for me as I deplaned, and after a short wait for my travel bags, we climbed in his car and headed out from the parking structure.

"I think we're going to have a good turnout tonight." Robert sounded eager.

"For what?"

"For your talk!"

"Tonight?"

"Yes ... we're running just a few minutes late. We'll be ok."

I groaned. "Robert, I've been awake for twenty-two hours."

We drove up to the Comfort Inn where he had booked a room for my talk. Inside, a large overflow crowd was waiting to hear me speak! All the seats were filled, people were sitting on the floor along the walls, and still more were coming in.

How am I going to make it through the next two hours with my energy dragging on the floor? Robert introduced me, and I took the floor. The audience was very receptive, and within a few minutes I felt totally energized. The evening ended on a high note with a full schedule for my first five days in the Motor City of the World.

Eight weeks later I was back in Detroit again with another full schedule of appointments. On the last day, Robert, Lynne and I were relaxing at the kitchen table before the ride to the airport. My bags were packed, and I'd soon be on my way to Chicago.

Robert had a sheaf of papers in his hand and was glancing through them.

"Malcolm," Robert said, "when I invited you here, I wasn't sure about you, but Lynne was, and she wouldn't take no for an answer."

"Robert thought his reputation as an A.R.E. speaker was at stake, if you weren't really good," Lynne chimed in from behind the kitchen sink.

"To ease my doubts, I made up these forms for people to fill out after their second session. The responses have really been impressive." He laid a few of the papers on the table for me to read while he continued looking through the rest.

A retired, 67-year-old Emergency Medical Services worker had come because of "floaters" — dust like particles swimming in the eye membrane. His eyes watered constantly and he had to wear sunglasses because of a high sensitivity to light. His ophthalmologist had compared his eyes to '…a windshield caked with smashed bugs and grit.' The floaters and other symptoms disappeared two days after his first session.

A spiritualist minister and psychotherapist came because of a chronic skin problem. In her report she wrote "I've tried everything for years, but nothing has worked. My skin began clearing up after my first session with Malcolm."

Persistent pain following eye surgery brought another woman to me. Her doctor dismissed the post surgery complication as a sinus condition that she would have to live with. After the first session, she noted, the pain disappeared completely.

Another woman testified that her spine had become "… as hot as if it were in a microwave oven." The heat, she said, was coming from inside the bone, not from my hands. As a teenager, she had been kicked in the back and suffered damage to her vertebrae. Over the years different chiropractors and osteopaths had treated her, but the problem persisted. Though she had come for another condition, and had not said anything about her spine to me, her back problems have improved since the first session.

Robert handed me another report from a lady with a persistent acid reflux condition producing symptoms resembling a heart attack. She had some noticeable improvements.

"She's a friend from church," Robert said. "She told me you had picked up information psychically about a baby she lost years before."

"I don't always get impressions or messages in my sessions," I answered, "and when I do, I don't always share them. I remember this lady. I told her that I saw a woman standing next to her holding a baby. At first I thought it was her mother, but she said her mother was still alive. So I said the woman may have been one of her guides or guardian angel. Then I asked if she had ever lost a baby, and she said yes. The lady seemed both surprised and comforted to know that the baby she had lost many years ago was in the loving hands of angelic beings."

Robert looked at me and asked the question that was always, somewhere, in the back of my mind.

"If you can do all this, why aren't you doing this full time?"

Robert knew my story. I had given him a copy of *Healer!* on the first visit. He was familiar with my misfortunes. So I didn't have to explain why I was working at Monckton Coke & Chemical.

"God will give me a sign if I am ever to do it again," I answered, "and I know what it is."

"What's the sign?"

"Have you ever heard of a Country and Western Singer called George Hamilton IV?" Robert responded with a yes. "Well, have you ever heard of an album called *Canadian Pacific*?"

"Oh, yeah, sure…" Robert attempted to hum a few bars. It was flat and off key, and mercifully he quit after a few seconds.

"It doesn't seem like that big a deal to find it."

"I've been looking for it for years, with no luck."

Robert reached for a phone directory, looked up a number and began dialing.

"W4 is the biggest Country and Western station around. I bet they have it."

Robert made his request to someone on the other end of the line. There was a brief pause, then he started writing down some numbers and hung up.

"The receptionist suggested I call the Golden Oldies station."

Robert punched in a new number. After a brief conversation, he hung up.

"They don't have it either."

I took a sip of coffee. It was starting to sound very familiar. I closed my eyes and thought about the plane ride to Chicago, not expecting much more from Robert.

"The receptionist told me to try this collector out in Brighton. She said he's got thousands of old, out-of-print tapes and records."

Robert tapped in a new number, made his request to whoever answered, and then waited with the phone to his ear. Suddenly he broke into a big smile.

"He's got it! We can go out and get it today."

I was startled and caught off guard. There was a rush of excitement instantly squelched by an anxiety attack. I was 53 years old, and to walk away from my job, even if it was a lousy one, made me very nervous. God calling in my contract? I didn't know if I was ready for this leap of faith.

"Robert, I've got a plane to catch."

"He says he can put it in the mail. Do you want it to go to England, or Chicago?"

"Have him send it here. I'll get it on the next trip."

I was still a little shaken and unsure how soon I wanted to seal the contract by accepting the album. I needed more time to adjust to the new circumstances.

"Now what are you going to do?" Robert said. His tone was enthusiastic and challenging.

I swallowed hard and said to Robert, "I guess the time has come for me to take a leap of faith."

I left Detroit still debating about stepping forward. I had asked for a sign, a small one, and got it. I had made a contract, and given my word. Now it was time to keep it. I was still struggling with two minds. But I knew a door had opened.

BACK AT MONCKTON COKE & CHEMICAL

On my first day back at work, the shop foreman called me off the floor.

"The boss wants to see you in his office."

That never feels like good news, I thought.

I tapped on the office door, and Mr. Williams, my boss, asked me to step in. He was sitting at his desk and motioned for me to come forward.

"Smith, we know what you're doing, and it's got to stop."

What's he talking about, I thought. I've got a good record. I work as hard as anyone here ... and I haven't taken sick days. Has someone got it in for me?

Williams flicked the ash from his cigarette to the floor and looked back at me.

"We give you all these days off with pay every month for one reason — so you don't get too exhausted and cause accidents at work. Now, you've got to decide what you want to do, because you can't be traveling to America and stepping off a plane and coming straight back to work. You're sure as hell going to hurt yourself or someone else. You can't do both."

He looked so serious, and I almost laughed out loud.

God couldn't have made it clearer if he wrote it in neon signs in the sky and signed it with thunder. Everything was crystal clear, with no possibility of misinterpretation. It boiled down to staying on the job and turning my back on God — or taking that leap of faith and giving up crabby bosses, long hours and an early grave.

I asked for a little sign, a cassette album. God gave me Monckton Coke & Chemical!

"Think it over, Smith, and let me know by tomorrow."

Two weeks later I put in my final hours at the plant and, with a giant grin on my face, punched the clock for the last time. It was January 1, 2000, the first day of a new year, a new century, a new millennium, and a new life as a full-time healer all rolled into one.

"Yes! I've done it," I said as I walked away.

And a little voice inside me said, "It's going to be all right."

And it has.

CHAPTER TEN

A CONVERSATION WITH MALCOLM

Compiled from interviews by Judith Pennington, Robert Krajenke and Pat Chalfant

Q: Each day you're scheduled for something like a 10-hour day doing healing — is that right?

Malcolm: A 12-hour day. Usually I get to take a half-hour break for lunch and then about an hour and a half for dinner. So it's a 10-hour working day.

Q: Do you work by instinct or do you believe you are really led?

Malcolm: To start with, I had to go to a Spiritualist Church to develop the gift. I was told by a psychic many years ago that I had the gift, but you have to develop it as you do with any gift. I went to a Spiritualist Church in England and they taught it the way they thought it should be done, which is that it needs to be a laying on of hands on the body. In different healing techniques, some don't actually touch the body, but it seems to be more potent when you do.

When I do touch the body, quite often the hands may be led into certain areas of the body that need extra time with the energy, and I do work, for sure, with guides or spirit doctors — whatever people feel comfortable calling them. So I just go with the flow on that one. The energy itself is from God but the application has got to be with the spirit doctors using God's energy and their knowledge of how to use it. I do truly believe that these spirit surgeons are angels who work with me on the spirit side of life, with the energy God provides.

Q: What does it take to become and be a healer?

Malcolm: I would say you've got to have an inner feeling for people, to want to help people and ease their suffering in any way you can. It comes down to love and compassion for your fellow man. Other than that, anyone can do it. It's like singing. But if you don't develop the gift, you don't get too far with it.

Q: You've said that you don't feel the energy passing through you during healings. What do you tune into at the beginning of the healing and what do you ask for?

Malcolm: I ask God to allow the person to receive healing. I also ask God that the guides be given the knowledge to overcome the problem the person has. The guides don't have healing energy of their own; they administer God's healing energy. So they have to work with their acquired knowledge. You can't have healing energy going into a body without intelligence to back it up. The guides need to know how to heal specific diseases, so they've got to acquire some knowledge from God to use that energy to overcome the problem. The closest example we have on this planet is the radiation given in hospitals. It's a very crude form of healing energy, but behind it is intelligence: the radiologist needs to know how much of it to use and for how long. The guides are using God's energy in the same way. If it were direct intervention by God, we would have 100 percent healing every time. We don't. We have 80 percent getting an improvement ranging from slightly improved all the way to 100 percent. You never know who's going to get what.

So, for the first few seconds, I pray and ask God to allow people to receive healing and to give knowledge to the guides working with me. Once I've said that, I listen to my music and enter an altered state. I know that my hands are moving around the body, but when I tell people things I don't remember them at all.

Q: What kinds of reactions do people have?

Malcolm: Some people just go out; they're gone. Some get emotional. Some sit and cry, even the men. Different people have different reactions, but almost everyone feels the warmth.

Q: Do you feel a sense of gratitude or wonder about this?

Malcolm: I'm still in amazement, because some days you get a major miracle, sometimes instantly, and sometimes it doesn't work for a pain in the elbow. You can cure a blind woman and not a person with floaters in the eyes. Here is my take on this. It's the same energy passing through me all the time, and that same energy has the same potential.

Q: Why does it work sometimes and not others?

Malcolm: Well, I never make guarantees or promises. I've had access to many big miracles on numerous occasions; but I'm no stranger to failure, either. God is the healer. Healers can't heal.

If a healing fails, there is always a reason for it. The reason is not always easy to understand. Frequently, a client experiences a removal of symptoms, but within a few days or weeks, the symptoms gradually return. Symptom relief means that only the physical level has been reached. The spirit needs to be touched by the healing energy. If it isn't, any physical improvement will only be temporary. When the soul is touched, there is always a change in consciousness or a new attitude toward life that accompanies the healing. When symptoms return, it doesn't mean the healing has failed, only that the cause of the illness is resisting the healing energy channeled through the healer.

There could be many reasons why a healing fails. It could be because the person is using the experience of the *problem* to teach somebody something; the spirit is saying, 'look, I need this, so I can't open up to receive it.' Sometimes, the person is throwing gasoline on the fire, so to speak, in subscribing to the problem. Sometimes the condition is karmic, so again it will not be relieved. Unless the spirit decides to let it go, if it's karmic you have a problem. Sometimes everything has to line up for a big miracle to come through.

Q: Can you give us some examples of "subscribing to the problem?"

Malcolm: I once treated a 78-year-old man for blindness. He came to me once a week for a couple of months. He would gain his vision back for four days, and then become blind until the next session three days later. After two months he stopped coming to me. He was getting suicidal because of the blindness. He'd rather have seven days of blindness, he said, than depression and partial vision.

At the same time, I was treating a neighbor every night for two weeks for tennis elbow without one iota of improvement. I discovered she worked on an assembly line, and the constant repetitive work of taking things off a conveyor was either causing or sustaining the problem.

In the case of the old gentleman, the cause of his blindness was his diabetes, which he refused to treat. The cause of my neighbor's problem was her job, which she didn't want to give up because the pay was good. A cure won't happen if a person subscribes to the same thing that causes the pain. Even when Spiritual Healing is successful, symptoms often return until the cause is completely overcome. The healing energy and the cause of the disease war with each other. In the beginning, the cause will win the battles, but in the end, if the person sticks with the process, the healing energy will win the war. So, unless you're willing to do your part, Spiritual Healing will give you limited results at best.

Q: Do you really feel as if you are stirring the soul?

Malcolm: Hopefully, anyhow. First of all, we are spirit in a body. We are here for soul growth and, at this stage of evolution, have to come into this physical body to experience that soul growth. When the time comes and we move to the spirit realm, there's another vehicle for the soul. Eventually, and many, many lifetimes away, the soul will not require a physical or spirit body as a vehicle. It will become pure energy and go back into the Godhead from whence it came.

The soul decides, to a point, anyway, whether the physical body heals. Everything is governed by universal law, even Spiritual Healing. If the need goes outside the law, like re-growing limbs, it won't happen.

Q: Do you sometimes have the experience of seeing these spirit people when they work with you?

Malcolm: No. Sometimes, I sense the spirit people who are with me, but most of the time, I don't. I'm not much of a "see-er" or very clairaudient. On a number of occasions, though, some of my clients have actually seen the main spirit surgeon who works with me. Now in the 23 years of doing the work, he has only been seen about 12 or 13 times by different people, but what makes it very interesting is that they all describe him exactly in identical detail — the way he dresses — even down to a piece of unusual jewelry he wears. You can't have different people over a 23-year time span coming in with exactly the same information without it being true information.

After gleaning the information from these people (and I never share the details with anybody) I know his name and the country he comes from. I know the way he dresses and in which era he lived. The reason I know this is that one lady years ago requested remote healing, which I sent her. One evening about 2 o'clock in the morning, she woke up and saw this man beside her bed. "Who on earth are you and what do you want?" she said. She thought he was somebody who had broken in. He told her his name and said "I've come to bring you peace." She replied, "Well, go away, go away." Once he realized that she was frightened of him, he was gone! So sometimes, if a client asks him a question, he will reply.

My daughter was the first to see him, though he never spoke to her. She was seven at the time. And then we have to go a few years before he was seen again. Again, the same dress, the same piece of jewelry, same exact details as my daughter described him. And another lady woke up — again in the small hours — and she said, "Who are you and where have you come from?" Again, he gave the same name and country as he did to the other lady years earlier. So gleaning this information, I know a lot about him.

Q: So, you feel this doctor is working with you?

Malcolm: When a person asks for distant healing to be sent to them, obviously, it is this great doctor, this great surgeon's role to go out to the individual to work with him, and often this great surgeon has been seen by these people making the request. They claim that he has appeared to them — materialized — and often has frightened the daylights out of them, but he usually appears to them because he's come to bring healing and he usually comes while they are in the sleep state in the middle of the night. So, occasionally, they have actually wakened up and have seen him.

Q: In the Spiritualist Church here in the U.S., as I said, people are taught to heal by moving their hands around the client as they feel moved to, instinctively. Is that different in the Spiritualist Church in England?

Malcolm: For the first six months of the classes in the Spiritualist Church in England, you are not allowed to actually touch the person and that's to weed out those who are really interested from those who are not. After six months the group of would-be healers usually dwindles from 13 or 14 down to maybe three. That's the first six months. They do explain to us that we do work with guides and the guides need us for a linkup between them and the client — to plug in the socket so to speak. You know, you've got the cable but you need the plug on the end of the cable or you can't make the connection.

Though the church I worked in did not say this to us, I've found out since that some churches tell you that you need permission to touch the body. Even if the person turns up for healing, and says,

"I've come for Spiritual Healing," you've still got to ask, "Is it okay if I put my hands on your body?" I believe in asking permission.

We are told that we, as healers, have got to have patience and so does the client. Again, some of these healers will drop out of the program because they have not got enough patience to see things through. If they don't have a healing or it's not happening after two or three visits, then they get tired and move on. Basically, you try to learn patience, and then each healer has to develop his own style and his own techniques.

Q: Do you do it in a sort of biofeedback way? That is, if something works with a certain client, or with a certain condition, then you do that again?

Malcolm: Yes. Instant miracles do happen, even for the big stuff. But usually, it's a slow progress. We learn to tell people that slow progress is better than no progress. In England, you usually get people going to healers only when the medical profession's failed them. Basically, we have to learn patience. We know that we are not doing the healing. We have to understand that we are not the healers.

We also sometimes have to have tolerance, too, because you're sometimes going to get people coming, occasionally Fundamentalists, for example, who will say, "If he is not healing through Jesus, then he's not going through God." You have to learn to tolerate these people. You have to learn not to argue with them. Basically, you just learn that spirituality comes in many forms, and some people have attitudes and you have to tolerate that.

Q: So you have to not let the client's belief system get in your way.

Malcolm: Right. That's for sure. Sometimes you get, for example, a wife coming along with her husband and the husband can be really negative about it all, but he's there because his wife is kind of attracted to it all and sometimes his negativity can really slow down the process, though it may not block the healing. Sometimes you have to sit down and explain things to the husband, he may not really believe in God.

Q: What do you do about that — the question of God?

Malcolm: Well, basically, just handle it with honesty. You've got to say, "Now, your wife is here because she's got a problem and all I'm trying to do is help her with that problem." Then all I can do is just do my best for them.

In England there have never been charges for healing. Most healers in England don't charge, so the guy knows that we're not trying to rip him off financially because it's free, anyway. So if you can just sit the guy down — even if sometimes he's arrogant — once he realizes that the purpose of the healer is just to help him out, it has a bigger effect than if you try to preach to the guy.

Q: You say the healing has to touch the soul. Can you explain?

Malcolm: Yes, the healing itself is funneled into the spirit and then it is transferred back to the physical body. It goes to the spirit first, and then it is transferred back to the physical. It is always the spirit itself that needs to be healed, it needs motivation, it needs to be stimulated and moved along spiritually on the pathway. Quite often the healing energy will do that — not always — but usually. In fact, there are some people who get healed spiritually, but not physically.

Q: By spirit, do you mean the aura?

Malcolm: No, the aura is a reflection of your spiritual well being. Basically, we are body, mind and spirit, and the physical body is the vehicle for the spirit to travel in while it's on the earth plane. When the physical body dies, the spirit becomes the vehicle for the soul. Eventually the soul will not require a physical body. Until then, the spirit within the physical body has to open and allow the energy to be taken in. If it doesn't open up or accept the energy for whatever reason, usually the healing will fail; it will be only a temporary effect if the spirit does not open up and take it on board. There can be many reasons why the spirit won't open up.

Q: What kinds of reasons?

Malcolm: For example, there's a big belief that when the spirit incarnates, we all come into the earth for a reason.

Q: Does this involve past lives?

Malcolm: Not necessarily past lives. It could be, but sometimes the spirit, before it incarnates, is shown a life plan of what awaits it and some of these spirits will take on the body of a diseased or deformed person and will use it for a teaching modality to teach something to somebody around it, like teaching patience. Or even the spirit itself may want the experience of being in the wheelchair to have that spiritual growth; but if that is the deal, the spirit will not open up. It will be saying, "Thank you very much for trying to help me, but I need this problem to teach somebody a spiritual lesson. I need to reject this energy because I need to complete my mission."

Sometimes the spirit has gone into hibernation, if you like, and it is not aware that the energy is there. It's like some people dying and they aren't even aware they are dead, but think that they still have life and they think they'll live forever and they don't accept their death. And sometimes the spirit will not accept that there is energy there waiting. Then there is karma — that it's not meant to be, but, as you know, karma can be ended in any lifetime.

But when you think about it, God is saying, "Look, you've asked for energy, you've gone to the healer, you're asking for divine help. I'm sending the energy on down, I don't want you to be ill, to suffer, so why not take it on board?"

Q: And that goes back to free will.

Malcolm: Free will and choice. We can choose to accept what God has to offer us or we can say, "No, thank you."

Q: What do you recommend that people do to test a spirit who is coming to them with information or healing?

Malcolm: Well, with regard to healing, all healing is from God. It is not from the devil as many people will have you think. You know, you get the Fundamentalists saying that these people are doing the devil's work and Jesus had the same accusations made to him and he came back with, "A house divided cannot stand." In other words, if the devil is going forward healing people of illness and even of possessing spirits, his house is not going to stand; he can't be doing God's work. I stopped arguing with the Fundamentalists, there's no use arguing with them.

Q: What about trance healers?

Malcolm: In England, the Spiritualist people always say, test the spirit. Don't be afraid to ask questions, such as, "If this is a true séance, can you tell me the name of my mother?" With clairvoyants, do the same thing. However, the healing speaks for itself.

Q: What can people do to develop healing powers if they don't have a class they can attend and they want to try to do healing?

Malcolm: First of all, they have got to have the desire and interest to follow through with their healing potential. Then they can do what I did. I started working on family members, just to know if I wanted to do this healing work. Every time that you place hands on a person there should be some progress, even if it's only slight progress. So, basically, you need to have a belief that the healing is coming from God. You must have a belief and faith that God is with you while you're doing the work. Then the motivation for doing the work has to be right, as well. If you're doing it because it's coming from the dollar sign, then it's not going to get very far; it's got to be coming from the heart.

Q: Are there any dangers that you can think of?

Malcolm: There will come a time, if the healer follows his gift, that he will start getting attention from the media and he will be asked to do radio interviews, TV interviews and newspaper item interviews and when he is doing these interviews, he'll find the media are only interested if he puts forward miracles. They're only going to mention the big miracles that have been brought through. They're not going to talk about failures, because the newspaper doesn't want to write about failures, just about miracles. So you're going to be mentioning miracles and when people see you on TV and hear you on the radio, all they're hearing is miracle, miracle, miracle, and then, as many people come forward full of hope, faith, full of belief — sometimes you have parents who bring a dying child to you — they've read your article and they think this is going to save their child! They give the child to you and it doesn't work and sometimes that can have a big negative effect.

Q: Is that hard on the healer?

Malcolm: It's hard on the healer, but it's even harder on the parents. I always tell the newspapers and magazines about failures, but the harmful side is that they don't want to report about negative stuff. They need to be pointing out that it doesn't work for everyone. Eventually, we do get it said that it doesn't work for everyone, but sometimes on radio and television, just before the program starts, they'll say, "We just need to hear the positive stuff."

Another good thing to know about energy work is, if the healing can't do any good it will leave the thing as it is. It won't do any harm.

Q: Is Spiritual Healing an alternative to orthodox medicine?

Malcolm: As powerful as Spiritual Healing is, it is not a replacement for orthodox medical care. It is complementary.

Q: Do you train healers?

Malcolm: Not really. I don't really have the time. I tell people just try and keep the healing simple. All you have to do is just put your hands on and let that energy flow; but, unfortunately, for lots of people, it's not simple, because it becomes too technical. It's also about the money. I've seen the advertisements in the magazines and sometimes they're paying hundreds and sometimes thousands of dollars to go on a week or two-week course to learn hands-on healing.

If that desire is with the person to heal other people, all you have to do is reach out and place hands on the person and let the energy flow. And, again, some healers will spend up to two hours (I know healers who spend two hours on one client) when the first ten minutes will bring through what it's going to bring through. Anything after that is purely psychological. The first ten minutes of the energy work is the time period that brings through on that day what it's going to bring through to improve them.

Q: Do you do anything special, such as meditate? Do you pray, do you follow any special diet?

Malcolm: In the morning when I go into the healing room, I say a brief prayer and ask God to give healing to all the people who come there and to give me strength to get through the day. That takes about 10 seconds. Then it's just hands on. People come in and I ask what the problem is and I tell them what to expect. I say don't expect instant miracles or guarantees that it's going to work. I'll do my best for you. Then I spend maybe twenty minutes with energy work (but the first ten minutes is the main factor). So the session does last half an hour with five minutes of talking, 20 minutes energy work, then another five minutes talking.

Then they usually have to wait two or three days for the energy they have been given to manifest itself into something positive. Usually, it takes about three days until the improvement. Some people are more receptive than others, with some people it's tomorrow, but with other people, it's next week. But most people have to wait three days. I've got a book of names and at night I pray over the book. There are too many names to pray for individually. I just ask God to give healing to the people listed in there. It has to be a prayer from the heart. If it's just casual, it won't work. It has to be a sincere prayer, each time, when you're asking God to give healing to the people — but basically, just keep it simple. If we just keep giving God the credit, we will succeed.

Q: If you were asked to define God, or explain what your idea of God was, what would you say?

Malcolm: That's a tough question because you're talking to a guy who left school at 15. What is God? Well, God is everything there is. God is love that brings happiness into a person's life. God is everything, everywhere and in everything. He is in you; he is in me. We're the same. In fact a question was asked Silver Birch, "When the time comes that we no longer need our spirit body, and that divine spark of divinity that came from God goes back to God, shall we lose our individuality when we "re-merge" with the God force?" Silver Birch came back and said, "Does a single note of a violin lose itself in a thousand-piece orchestra? Or does the wave lose itself in the ocean?" And he said, "No. Although you have "re-merged," you will still be who you are."

Q: Do you have any relationship with Jesus, the master healer?

Malcolm: Not apart from the fact that I get quite a few people experiencing him during the healing. My question is, how do you know you've seen him, because nobody knows what he looks like! (laughter).

Q: How would you advise others to develop their healing gifts?

Malcolm: With love, compassion, simplicity. That's all you need. And perhaps a little bit of patience.

CHAPTER ELEVEN

FINAL THOUGHTS ON HEALING

Healers don't heal, God does!

FIVE THINGS TO KNOW ABOUT SPIRITUAL HEALING

1. MIRACLES HAPPEN

A small percentage of people experience great, wonderful healing miracles, but this is not the norm. Spiritual Healing is a process, not a shortcut. Over 80% of people receiving Spiritual Healing will see gradual improvement over a time if they stay consistent with their process.

2. SYMPTOMS CAN BE RELIEVED, BUT THE CAUSE MUST BE HEALED

It is not uncommon for people who experience a healing to have their symptoms return. This doesn't mean the healing has failed, only that the cause of the illness is resisting the healing energy. The cause of the illness and the healing energy are in opposition to each other, and frequently the cause wins the battle. If the client is patient and persistent, the higher vibrations of the healing energy will eventually transform the dis-ease and discomfort and produce permanent healing.

3. THE SOUL MUST BE TOUCHED

The primary objective of Spiritual Healing is not to heal the physical body, but to stir the soul. When Spirit touches the soul, there is always a change in consciousness, a shift in perception and attitude that accompanies the healing energy and allows it to manifest.

4. NOTHING IS GUARANTEED

The purpose for our illness and distress is not always understood. Conditions may be karmic in origin, and cannot be released until the soul lesson is learned. In other cases, highly evolved souls often voluntarily choose an illness, disease or defective body in order to give others opportunities to learn lessons through their relationship to them. Ask any parent with a severely handicapped child or loved one, "What have you learned from your loved one being disabled?" and most often they will tell you ... "Patience," "Compassion," "Unconditional Love," "Depth of Being," or other qualities of the eternal self. In these cases, the soul being prayed for will reject rather than accept the healing energy when it is not in alignment with the soul's mission or purpose.*

5. THE HEALING ENERGY COMES FROM GOD

Healers do their part by offering to be a channel for God's healing energy to flow. The person receiving the energy does his or her part by being receptive and allowing the energy in. The energy is directed by specialists (aka angels) in the spiritual world. *Only God can heal. God is the healing energy.* This is true whether it comes from prayer, laying on of hands, herbs, manipulation, surgery, placebos or prescription drugs. All healing comes from God.

---

* There is a growing trend that I encounter in my travels, and this is the admonition not to pray for others because it will interfere with their karma. The thought behind this is that some souls have a mission and, in order to give others opportunities to learn lessons, will take on an illness or addiction, or get born into situations where terrible abuse occurs. In Chicago, there was a woman who began

to telephone all the prayer groups, telling them to stop sending out prayers because it would interfere with karma.

A few months later, her son was in a terrible car accident and straight away she started calling all the prayer groups in the area, asking them to pray for him. I don't think anyone in those groups was concerned about interfering with his karma. No matter how much prayer energy is directed at a soul, the soul decides to accept or reject the healing energy. If a soul has come in to teach or learn a lesson by taking on an illness or a defective body, then the soul will not accept the energy directed at it in prayer. The only damage prayer can do is to the gates of hell.

Most people regard pain and suffering as misery, yet sickness and suffering have their role in the evolution of a person, depending upon their maturity.

In 1984 there was a huge famine in Ethiopia. On the evening news, an American journalist was interviewing an Ethiopian man at a Red Cross Food Station where thousands of people lay stretched out on the ground, dying, starving, and sick. The man was emaciated and weak and could hardly stand. He had walked 300 miles from his village to get food. Along the way his wife and child both died in his arms. The journalist asked this man if he believed in God, and the Ethiopian said, yes. He believed in God before the famine, believed in God while he walked, and still believed now.

"Why do you think God is punishing Ethiopia," the journalist asked as the camera panned over rows and rows of dying, starving people.

"It is not a punishment," the Ethiopian replied with one of the most poignant, profound answers I have ever heard. I can still see him clearly against that backdrop of misery. And this is what he said, "The people of Ethiopia have come together as one soul to test the compassion and humanity of the planet."

So, there's the answer. Why there is so much pain and suffering is a great mystery. When we embrace it, it just might heal the soul.

APPENDIX 1

TESTIMONIALS - HEALING STORIES

BABY KATIE

Roche Bentley, Cambridgeshire, England

In 1987, we welcomed Katie into the world. After only two weeks she was rushed to Great Ormond Street Children's Hospital with a transposition of the arteries and a ventricle septic defect. Basically that means that her heart arteries were the wrong way round, a fault affecting two thousand babies in Britain each year; and more seriously, that she had holes in her heart and her right ventricle was too small for a corrective operation. Immediate surgery extended her life by a few days but the doctors and nurses held out little hope as Katie was becoming weaker and weaker and was not expected to survive an operation. Nevertheless the doctors agreed to try and an operation was planned. On the Saturday before the operation I remembered that our good friends Bill and Isobelle Donaldson had mentioned that they had a friend who was a healer. In desperation we telephoned Bill and Isobelle and they promised to contact their friend ... Malcolm Smith.

On Sunday Bill and Malcolm drove to Cambridge in Bill's car and I met them at our home. I drove them to the hospital and on the way Malcolm asked me if I had brought the handkerchief he had requested. I passed it to him and he held it between his hands. He also told me that he had asked for absent healing on Katie the previous night at about 10 p.m. He said that it was a possibility that Katie would have become agitated around that time.

When we entered the intensive care ward, Katie was fast asleep in her special cot. The wires and tubes connected her to various machines and it was clear to everyone that our baby was very weak indeed. Malcolm immediately placed his hands over the baby's body. He didn't actually touch Katie, his hands hovered above. As Malcolm held his hands above Katie he asked a nurse to look up Katie's records. He inquired if Katie had shown signs of distress at around ten to ten-thirty the night before. The nurse checked and was surprised. Katie had woken and had sweated profusely, she had been upset and didn't settle for some time. Malcolm explained to Tricia (my wife) that he had been trying some absent healing.

After about ten minutes Malcolm stopped and turned to Tricia. He gave her the handkerchief and said that in about ten minutes Katie would become distressed again and that Tricia should touch Katie with the handkerchief.

Finally, Malcolm told me that he would be going as it was a long way back to Yorkshire. I had promised to take Malcolm and Bill back to their car in Cambridge and was about to leave. Katie then started to wake and to sweat but Malcolm touched her with the handkerchief and she immediately stilled.

Suddenly, and it was really very sudden, Tricia burst into tears. The change was stunning and water actually poured from her eyes as if from two taps. Malcolm placed his hands on Tricia's head. It was like someone had flicked a switch. Tricia changed completely and sat down, her face totally drained, and she was silent. The change was remarkable.

Malcolm looked at me and asked me to get the operation planned for Katie delayed. He said that Katie would get worse and become weaker but that Wednesday would see an improvement and she would get stronger. He implied that an operation would have a better chance if it could be postponed until Wednesday next or possibly later. I didn't see how I could have any effect on the doctors' decision as to when to operate and I expected a difficult time with the registrar.

The response to my request was quick in coming. The decision was that there was little hope and that waiting a day or so would not make much difference to the inevitable outcome.

On Monday, Katie's condition worsened and on Tuesday she was still very weak. She had constant nursing and Tricia and I never left her except to snatch some sleep. On Wednesday Katie seemed to improve and her graph results were going up instead of creeping down. By Wednesday afternoon Katie was quite lively. On Thursday afternoon Katie was improving further, and on Friday there was a cancellation in the theater and Katie had her operation. Not only did she survive it but the surgeon was absolutely delighted with the lung pressures and other results. Katie improved further and following a small operation to test the effects of the major surgery, Katie was soon moved to a less intensive care ward, and we were looking forward to going home.

Did Malcolm Smith heal Katie? All I can say is that her condition was very poor; it was steadily deteriorating and we were given little hope. The priest had baptized her and administered the Last Rites. We had the best hospital care in the world and scores of people saying prayers. We even had holy medals hanging on the cot. It looked like a small shrine and all the nurses respected the sanctity of Malcolm's special handkerchief. I do know that I wouldn't hesitate to call on Malcolm or to request the assistance of any other healer.

Yes, I can honestly say that Malcolm's care and gift has helped Katie and our family tremendously, and I thank God for Malcolm Smith and his healing gift.

***

IRREPARABLE VISION LOSS RESTORED

Lynne Browning-Krajenke

My mother was slowly going blind. Glaucoma and cataracts had reduced her vision to the point where she constantly complained that things in her apartment were lost, stolen or missing. She simply couldn't see well enough to recognize them.

My mother is an independent, tough-minded woman who for many years was used to traveling cross country by herself in her ancient 1972 converted Chevrolet van. At age 73, still attractive and feisty, she has been alternately diagnosed with dementia and Alzheimer's. In one moment, she is fully engaged, interacting with family and friends. In the next breath, it's all forgotten. Some days she appears energized and full of herself; other days, there is only a shadow of the woman I know as my mother. If my mother went blind, I knew she would quickly deteriorate and die. After so many losses, it would be the final straw.

The ophthalmologist, a geriatric vision specialist at Henry Ford Hospital, told us the optic nerve in her right eye was so deteriorated that it wasn't worth an operation. However, he agreed to operate on her left eye, and forewarned us that her vision would not improve. The cataract removal would simply clear up what little vision she had. The specialist explained that glaucoma surgery consists of making a hole in the back of the eye to drain off excess fluids. Removing the cataracts will raise the pressure in the eye, he said, and the increased pressure could result in the loss of what vision she had remaining in her left eye. The doctor also explained that there was no known medical intervention to heal the optic nerve. Her vision could not be repaired beyond the 20/80 she now possessed in her best eye.

In other words, she was faced with a 50% chance of going blind as a result of the surgery she needed! And surgery, according to the doctor, was the only procedure he could offer to prevent further damage to the optic nerve.

My mother was one of the first to experience Malcolm on his initial visit to Detroit. Two days after her session, she went to have the cataracts on her cornea measured. Later, at home, when the effects of the numbing medication wore off, she began to experience stabbing pain in her eye. We called the Emergency Room at Henry Ford Hospital and were urged to bring her in immediately. They suspected a glaucoma escalation was occurring.

Four painful and anxious hours later, we were informed that her cornea had been scratched when the measurements on her cataracts were made. The medication had exacerbated the wound and increased the pain. By 1:30 a.m. the pain had subsided enough where I felt comfortable leaving her alone in her apartment. I urged her to call me if there were any problems, and I promised to see her first thing in the morning.

The following morning, her eyes still hurt. She couldn't keep them open without pain. With her eyes closed, the discomfort lessened, but there was still noticeable pain. Since her eyes weren't responding as expected, her ophthalmologist advised against further medication. I brought mom back to my house, where Malcolm was treating his clients.

Malcolm seemed acutely aware of her discomfort and asked if he could work with her between other scheduled appointments. Mom jumped at the opportunity! Malcolm treated her for about three minutes and then went down the stairs to his next appointment. Relief was immediate! Over the next few hours, Malcolm took several more opportunities to treat her. By the end of the day, all traces of her pain were gone.

Because of mother's progress under Malcolm's care, I wanted her to have another session with him before her eye surgery. I also knew she would be receiving absent healing during the interim until Malcolm returned in six weeks.

On our next visit, I asked the ophthalmologist if we could postpone the surgery until mid-December. I attributed the delay to problems with my schedule as a psychotherapist. He was satisfied her medication was maintaining her eye pressure at a safe level, so he cautiously agreed to the delay.

Malcolm returned on December 8th, and mom had her next session the following afternoon. Five days later, she went in for surgery. I visualized ministering angels surrounding her, the surgeon, and everyone else involved with the procedure. I filled the operating room with brilliant white light, and released it all into God's Hands. The surgery lasted an hour and a half. When the doctor returned to the waiting room he had the look and stance of a man with good news. "The surgery couldn't have gone better," he announced with great satisfaction. Silently, I expressed my appreciation to Malcolm, his guides and all the ministering angels. Then I thanked the doctor for his excellent care!

Three days later at one of her post-op appointments, a nurse was testing my mother's vision and checking her eye pressure and vision.

Her brow furrowed as she studied the results. Concerned, I asked if something was wrong. "No," she said, "not a thing."

She left the room and a few moments later, the doctor came in and repeated the identical tests. As he reviewed the findings, he was obviously puzzled. My stomach tightened. Her field vision test instantly flashed across my mind. The test had shown almost total darkness and very little light!

"Is there a problem?" I asked.

"No problem at all," he responded. "In fact, everything is fantastic."

Her vision had been corrected from 20/80 to 20/30 — an improvement that he earlier said was impossible. He and I were equally amazed! Not only had she been saved from going blind, but her eye was restored to almost perfect vision! And on our subsequent visit, we discovered her eye had improved even more! The healing energy was still active and working on her!

Mom knows she will have to work with her doctor and continue taking her medications to ensure that the glaucoma she has doesn't destroy the newly repaired optic nerve. Does she believe in Spiritual Healing? You bet! Does she believe the glaucoma can be 100% healed? Why not?

Spiritual Healing conjures up different images, different explanations and expectations for most of us. Some have faith. Many want to believe. Others are skeptics. For those who experience it, Spiritual Healing is a deeply personal experience, and remembered in different ways. For my mother, Spiritual Healing will always be a light shining through the darkness, made possible through the healing touch of Malcolm Smith. And Malcolm, who has been the agent for thousands of healings, simply says in his unassuming way, "God is the healer, not me. I am just a physical instrument He works through."

Lynne Krajenke is a psychotherapist with a private practice in the Greater Metropolitan Detroit area and specializes in a wide range of alternative therapies.

APPENDIX 2

THE BOOK OF TESTIMONIALS

The following testimonials represent a small sample of the scope and variety of experiences people have received during their sessions with Malcolm. First name and last initial are used in respect of the privacy of the person. When possible, the date and location are listed.

A.R.E. NEW YORK CENTER

J. S. - New York, NY, April 3, 2000

When I first attended a lecture by Malcolm Smith in November 1999, he asked to demonstrate healing for anyone who had severe pain. I had the privilege to be one of several who were selected. I told him I had a knife-like pain on my spine between my shoulder blades. I've had many injuries to my upper back over several years and until that date had numerous attacks to that area which MRIs showed had a slight tear of soft tissue and scoliosis. I sat comfortably on a soft chair in front of Malcolm Smith and he placed his warm, soothing hands over my upper spine. With gentle swaying accompanied with heavenly music, he applied various shaking hand manipulations. The pain seemed to float out of my body into an endless ocean and has never returned since.

Celeste S. - New York, NY

I came to watch a sample healing at Malcolm's Friday night lecture. While he was healing someone in the front of the room, I felt energy run down my arms and since then I have reduced arm and wrist pain. I am freer from this pain than I've been in eight years. I am looking forward to my private session.

Celeste S. - June 10, 2000, Second Session

Since my last session 80% of my arm pain is gone. Time has passed and I've had time to process what happened last time. For no apparent reason I started to cry and a white light came over me that was so beautiful and full of love that I almost couldn't bear it. The contrast of such all-knowing, unconditional love versus my closed hard heart was drastic. Something has opened since then which I can't explain. Malcolm is a true healer in many ways.

Liz E. - Mamaroneck, NY, January 1, 2001

I've seen Malcolm two times. The first time it was snowing in the spring. I enjoyed the session and felt relaxed but I didn't notice any large changes in the conditions I sought his help for - tinnitus, left hand pain, emotional pain. During the second session two months later Malcolm asked me about my hand. I told him it was an injury I suffered twenty-five years earlier from a circular saw in which I cut three fingers to the bone and almost lost my hand. I had frequent periods of pain that caused me much suffering. I had learned to cope with it until last year when it became quite severe and nothing seemed to ameliorate this pain. I sought the advice of a top hand surgeon and hand therapist and spent a year doing exercises to prepare for the surgery that was a possible partial cure for the contractures and scar tissue and arthritis in my left hand. I was continuing on this path until my hand therapist herself suffered a bad injury.

About this time, I was in a car struck by a mail truck. I had other pains to heal and so I put the hand treatment on the back burner, until Malcolm saw me that second time. Malcolm kept looking at my hand. I told him there was probably nothing he could do. It was an old injury. I had learned to live with it for so many years and I didn't see how energy healing could change the structural changes and contractures in my hand. Besides my tinnitus was acting up. I really wanted that fixed first. So much for my controlling the healing process! Malcolm kept looking at my hand, stroking it and placing his healing energies into it. I felt relaxed at the conclusion of the session, but I did have some nausea. I was anxious to go home. When I got home I developed a severe headache and vomited for hours. The healing session seemed so far away. The violent nausea and vomiting finally ended many hours later. When it was over I noticed for the first time in so many, many years that my consciousness was not drawn to my hand. This was amazing - the pain had gone away. Something I did not even imagine was possible! Thank you!

Phyllis R. - New York, NY, January 18, 2003

Today is my third session with Malcolm for severe migraine headaches. These usually occurred the week before my period. After session two (I didn't even want to say it!) but the pain and pressure I usually felt had subsided tremendously! I previously missed many days of work because of my condition, but now hardly ever need to call in sick. Thank you, Malcolm, from the bottom of my heart for helping to give me my health back.

Shorter testimonials from the A.R.E. New York Center:

Joan S.

For thirty years, I had chronic Irritable Bowel Syndrome with fifteen internal hemorrhoids causing heavy bleeding. After Malcolm Smith's healing session, I have had normal functioning and no hemorrhaging or pain again.

Marilyn E.

I came to Malcolm due to a flashing in my right eye. I have been to the Eye Hospital in Manhattan. They could not find the cause of it. After seeing [Malcolm] three times, my eye is completely better.

Jesse G.

I have Muscular Dystrophy, which causes progressive weakening of the muscles. Since I have been seeing Malcolm, I have had some improvement in my breathing and cardiac functioning as measured by medical testing. I have often felt a sense of euphoria and well being after treatments.

Marie C.

I had fragments of a large kidney stone for more than twelve years. Malcolm has treated me at least eight times, and the number of fragments diminished, so that at present there are very few as evidenced by x-rays.

A.R.E. CHICAGO CENTER

Sandra R. - Davenport, IA, November 1, 2001

My trouble has been weakness in my left leg causing me to fall on many occasions. This condition is from an earlier childhood illness. The leg still remains weak and I still occasionally fall. What is different is that I no longer fear the fall. Malcolm's treatments have helped to eradicate the fear. Before when I fell, I would become tremendously frustrated, upset, angry and worried about becoming a helpless invalid. I no longer fear the fall or become emotional afterwards. I have also learned to fall without pain. Perhaps, in time the physical symptoms will disappear. For now I am grateful for the emotional healing and the lessons I have learned from these experiences. Thank you Malcolm. I will be seeing you again.

Jerry L. H. - Davenport, IA, January 10, 2002

I first came to Malcolm in September 2001. I was hopeful for a healing of an aspect of terror that had consumed my life. My healing felt warm and safe, gentle and protected. My trust and feeling of safety from Malcolm was immediate. He seemed like an earth angel. A few times I felt uncertain whether I was sitting in the chair or floating in air. At the end of the session Malcolm asked me if I was aware of a terrorist attack coming to the U.S. from men whose hearts were full of evil. He said he felt it was very near but I should not be frightened and that it would be good to have extra water and food on hand.

Since my first and second healing, I have felt terror unravel in my life. I've been able to look at the incidents leading to the terror and remember without real fear. I feel blessed to have met Malcolm.

Pat A. - Chicago, IL, March 22, 2002, First Healing

Through the good Lord I was blessed and healed by Malcolm at his lecture. I have been ill with gastro paresis, gastro reflux, and depression for about one year and four months — constant pain, fatigue, nausea and more. I felt like I had been missing out on life. When Malcolm laid his hands on me the heat was overwhelming and I felt energy flowing through my body from my head to my toes. People in the room watched the change in my face from beginning to end and noticed the difference immediately. It was like a bolt of lightening. My hands, normally cold, were warm and tingly. I felt energized and great! No pain from Friday the 22nd to Tuesday 3/26. I gained one and a half pounds, ate food I couldn't eat before, went to the bathroom normally, was energized and there was no feeling of depression. I was actually happy. My blood pressure is better and my pulse rate is 68 from 92. Saw Malcolm again on March 26, 2002. The sensation was much different - less shocking, more of a comforting heat almost like a child being held by its mother. My hands again are warmer and I feel a touch on my heart. I didn't tell him I had a slightly sore throat and that went away too.

Jennifer S. - Chicago, IL, April 14, 2002, Second Visit

On my first visit, January 14, 2002, I came to see Malcolm complaining of a severe, recurrent pain in my left hip. (Actually, running from my lower left side to mid-thigh.) During our session I felt warmth where Malcolm placed his hands. Afterwards, I went home and took a nap. I also slept with the handkerchief that Malcolm had blessed as he had instructed, close to my side and tucked in the bottom of my pajamas. After a week the pain was completely gone and I remain pain free.

Nancy G. - Chicago, IL, Third Healing

A mass in my liver has disappeared! I feel much more at peace about marketing my book inspired by Jesus' ideas, concepts and images. I was afraid of taking the next step, but now feel much more peace and can allow myself to be lead by Spirit more consistently.

Ruth N. - Chicago, IL

Words are insufficient to describe how my life has improved since receiving healing through Malcolm. I had a ruptured disk in my back and after just two visits it was healed and I came home and cleaned my carpets. That was five years ago and the pain has never returned. I also developed a "frozen" shoulder that made the slightest movement very painful. By the end of the fourth visit I had full motion, pain free. That was three years ago and it has not returned. But most important is what has healed below the surface, never to be seen. Words are insufficient.

Myron M. - Chicago, IL

After my first visit I felt relief in just a few weeks. The ringing in my ears stopped and the pressure in my sinus went away. The semi-sharp pains in my lower back became less frequent over the next few months. After nearly a year, I am still feeling healed and will continue to seek Malcolm's help.

Linda G. - Davenport, IA

I brought my 8-year-old border collie, King, to Malcolm because his health started to fail, his coat was dull and he was loosing hair, falling down stairs and scratching continuously. He even seemed depressed. I brought him to Malcolm, and after the third day, no symptoms. I held the hanky on him every night for three nights 'til I fell asleep. Now his coat is shiny, he's healthy and happy. I would do it again in a heartbeat.

Christine J. - Davenport, IA

This is my third visit with Malcolm. After my second visit I had almost immediate healing of a surgical area. I had surgery to remove an ovarian cyst. I presented the surgeon with a nasty surprise. I had a massive infection, an abscess on my colon that was also starting to infect my bladder. The surgeon had to remove 22 inches of my colon and gave me a colostomy. Because this was not planned and

I was not healing, I had to go in for a second surgery to revise the colostomy. The surgeon used stronger, long-lasting stitches but I still did not heal. Within three days of seeing Malcolm after the second surgery the whole surgical area was healed. The surgeon was very surprised, but happy. So was I.

A.R.E. HOUSTON CENTER

Liz M. - Houston, TX, February 4, 2002

Since 1984 I have been on hormone replacement therapy that resulted in migraine headaches lasting three days and occurring every one to two months. I first saw Malcolm about a year ago for this problem. After my first session I was sitting in a chair but I began to have such a tremendous surge of energy, I had to get up and walk around. Today was my fifth session, and I have remarkable improvement. According to my calendar, I have not had a headache lasting more than 23 hours since July 2001. None of the headaches I've had since that first session has been debilitating like the ones I used to have.

Melissa S. - El Paso, TX

I could not even turn my neck without severe pain in my back. This had been a problem for several weeks and was not its worst when I came to see Malcolm. In one 25-minute session, my pain was completely gone. I could move again! I have suffered from depression and anxiety for the past 10 years — I had just been through a serious bout of depression and anxiety when I came to see Malcolm. The same day I saw him I felt peace and calm. This feeling lasted close to a month. I have seen Malcolm again today and know my depression and anxiety is going away.

Barbara R. - El Paso, TX

I came in September for healing of my immune system and my emotional body as well. I am 3/4th there now as of January 24, 2002. I am also receiving healing on my eyesight and my mind, body, emotions and spirit. I have seen colors and divine white light. I have seen Jesus in splendid light. I have been healthier since I first came to see Malcolm and I am getting stronger and especially soul-contented. I will continue to heal and see Malcolm and be blessed by God.

Celeste L. - El Paso, TX

During my first session I felt a warmth and vibration and strong sense of love and safety. Afterward, Malcolm told me that my dad had passed away about three years ago, which I had not told him. It was absolutely true. I will continue to see him.

I was taking two different medications for blood pressure and still ran a high pressure. After seeing Malcolm my pressure is now normal or low and I hope to go off meds.

THE HERITAGE STORE, VIRGINIA BEACH, VA

Kay S.

After having a liver transplant, my daughter Kelly's immune system was basically shot from all of the medications she was required to take to prevent organ rejection. A few months later found her covered with warts, a hundred or more of them. She was 13, and at a difficult age to deal with all of that. She was living in Florida with her Dad. I went to Malcolm at the Heritage Center here in Virginia Beach, and he prayed and gave me a handkerchief infused with healing for Kelly - to put under *my* pillow. The next day I called to tell her that I had been to Malcolm, at which point she declared that the night before all of her warts had disappeared. Her father got on the phone and confirmed it with great amazement. It was a stunning victory on behalf of Malcolm's gift of remote healing.

WING RETREAT CENTER, PARIS, TENNESSEE

My name is **Barbara H. Bramlett of Paris, Tennessee** and I am giving you permission to use my name and testimonial in any future publications and including the book. Malcolm is a dedicated 'Instrument of God.' I was lacking in the physical aspect of my life and urged to attend his first session in this area. Being skeptical, I refused the first call but consented the last day. My physical condition consisted of a thirty-year bout with heart and attendant problems.

And, an eye glass wearer for forty years. I was fine in the other three conditional categories. As an afterthought, I included the eyes for evident healing. I also included the spine.

My recent third session found me reading the newspaper print the third day after my session. Remarkable! I am certain I am returning to normal in the other areas also. I have a physical scheduled the latter part of July and will see the results then. I am totally out of my glasses. I noticed his 'hot' healing hands and a hot fluid of energy rushing down my spine more than once. I am certain the results will be permanent.

My most significant experience with Malcolm is the evident healing of the eyes and the kind energy he expends during the visit. I have always been a skeptic in the past but totally convinced that this is a gift from God. Barbara H. Bramlett.

A.R.E. SOUTHERN CALIFORNIA CENTER

Tim L. - San Rafael, CA, February 11, 2002

This has been my fourth visit. After my second visit, a chronic pain in my left shoulder (lasting for ten months) has left. I can move my left arm totally without pain. My asthma has diminished and my anxiety of living has been removed. Having AIDS, my numbers have been excellent, even being off the toxic medications. Malcolm truly is a gift from God.

Kevin B. - Chino, CA, November 26, 2002

I was diagnosed with Congestive Heart Failure in December 1998. My symptoms slowly worsened over the span of 3½ years. In March of 2002 my health had deteriorated to the point that my heart specialists believed I would require a heart transplant.

In April 2002 I was treated by Malcolm Smith for the first time. A dramatic improvement in the condition of my heart and general health followed. This improvement has been substantiated by various medical tests.

As of today's date, Malcolm Smith has treated me on four occasions. I believe these treatments have given me a new lease on life. I would most fervently recommend the healing treatments of Malcolm Smith to any person with a health problem of any sort.

Connie T. - San Jose, CA

Before I came to Malcolm, I just had a lumpectomy for breast cancer. It was the aggressive type called ductal carcinoma. The cancer cells were to the margin and may have penetrated to the rest of the breast. I came to Malcolm and when the surgeon went back into the breast to take out more, the lab said there was no more cancer. Praise God and thank you, Malcolm.

Richard D. - Redwood City, CA

Within seconds my heartaches disappeared. Very smooth. Every time he puts his hands on me it feels like a blowtorch. I love it!

Randy T. - Monrovia, CA

Malcolm is not a tall, big, imposing person. He's soft spoken and gentle. My impression of Malcolm jelled after a long thought about it after we had met. I finally realized that Malcolm is the sort of person I had always visualized Jesus Christ being … and that's why he seemed familiar to me at our very first meeting.

At the time I visited him, I had previously had three heart attacks. When I went to see Malcolm, my good friend who accompanied me, assumed that I would be discussing my heart condition and physical health. Instead, after Malcolm asked me, "How can I help you, Randy?" I explained that I had been unemployed for the better part of seven months and needed to find a good job with benefits. Malcolm and I sat in silent prayer. Then as I sat with my back to him, eyes closed, he began a slow touch beginning at the top of my head, and moving down to my torso. During this time, I had a vision of Jesus. Then of the Virgin Mary, with a scarf over her head. As Malcolm embraced me from behind, he became my vision of the Virgin Mary embracing me; then the Virgin became my mother, who had died in my youth. Mom smiled at me and said softly as she often had, "Don't worry honey, everything's going to be okay." Then the vision evaporated. We sat silently at the end of the session, then I opened my eyes and turned around. I burst into tears when Malcolm

167

said, "Your mother was here … at least I think it was your mother — she has your eyes."

Malcolm said that I would have a job within two weeks, but I should get word about the job within three days. He gave me his blessing and I left there feeling wonderful. My friend said I looked "younger" and I did. I felt younger too, like I was walking on air. My meeting with Malcolm was Wednesday. When I arrived home, there was a message on the answering machine from a prospective employer to whom I had sent my resume. The man explained in the message that he'd been busy so he hadn't had a chance to contact me until now. It was too late to contact him that night, so I called Thursday morning. We talked about the job. There was a hiring freeze on until the end of the year (it was near Thanksgiving time). I suggested I work as a consultant under contract until the new year. We'd both have a chance to look each other over. He agreed, and faxed some paperwork to me, which I filled out.

The next day I took my drug test and I was officially a consultant. On Friday after I had prepared my suit and was ready to begin the new job on Monday, I sat on the bed and heard Malcolm's reassurances about having a job within three days. A sense of relief, of joy, of blessing simultaneously washed over me. I felt very close to God in that moment. I performed well in the job, the company hired me, and I've been with them almost two years now, with full benefits and retirement, making more money than I've ever made in my life. On my desk is a photo of Malcolm, a constant reminder that my job and everything that flows from it is a gift from God.

I had a second session with Malcolm about two months later. My most significant experience with Malcolm was the re-affirmation of my own worthiness of God's love. Sometimes in the day-to-day hustle and bustle of just getting through the day, I would take for granted that each day is a blessing and comes with the promise of wonderful things great and small.

Malcolm gave me new eyes to see this with and I have a greater awareness now. It's funny because I've always been somewhat of a skeptic, mainly because I wasn't exactly sure what it was all about. I've learned that spiritual, mental, emotional, physical, and financial health are all tied together, and it is a matter of balance … like the mouse-eared balloon — squeeze down one ear and the other ear gets bigger. An out-of-balance condition in one area reflects in other areas. And so with my Spiritual Healing. I truly received a healing of my spirit, but all the other areas of my health benefited as well.

A.R.E. SOUTHERN FLORIDA

A.R.E. Coordinator Mary Ann Denn, August 2004

We had a wonderful experience here with one of Malcolm's people. She had been told to go home and have fun because there was nothing else for them to do for her. She had a fast spreading melanoma and a heart condition. Before she left after her second healing, Malcolm had suggested she go to her doctors before she came again. She came in ecstatic. Her doctors had said they could find no sign of cancer and that her heart was fine. We had others who also were much better and improved.

DETROIT, MI
UNEXPLAINED MALCOLM MYSTERIES FILE:
RED HOT BATTERY

Janice Sparks - South Lyon, MI

Thursday evening, I came with my husband, brother, and niece for healings. I hung my coat over the back of the couch. In my pocket I had a camera battery that had gone "zonk." I took it with me the day before to buy a new one and I wanted to make sure I bought the right one. On our way home after the healings we stopped at the pharmacy to pick up some things. As I was leaving I reached into my pocket and something burned my hand. It was so hot I quickly pulled out my hand and ran to the truck. When I got in, I told my husband and reached in and pulled it out, bouncing it up and down because it was so hot. It was the camera battery.

We couldn't figure it out. It was a bad battery and it wasn't hooked up to anything — no connection at all. It stayed hot for about five or six hours and cooled gradually. Then it dawned on me that my jacket was hanging right at the hallway, across from the room where Malcolm Smith was doing the healings. So after I talked to you I put that "bad" battery in the camera and it worked great! So I am leaving it there. Like you said, it might last forever, ha ha ha!

APPENDIX 3

A HEALER ASKS FOR PRAYER

As a healer for the past 25 years, I have sat almost on a daily basis watching the miracles come and go. Some have been awesome - vision restored, blindness healed, inoperable cancer cured -- and others not as dramatic, but just as heartening as those for whom the orthodox medical profession could do no more - depression lifted, hope restored, and lives changed. In all those years, I never thought I would want one myself, but in the Spring of 2004, it was my turn to ask for a miracle - not for myself, but for my son Karl.

Karl lives at home with his mum and I. A loner, he spends much of his time in his room, keeping to himself. On Sunday morning, April 25th, just four weeks before his 30th birthday, Karl came down the stairs complaining of tremendous pain in his foot. The pain, he said, was unbearable. Kathleen, my wife, asked him to take his socks off. What she saw shocked her! His left foot was completely black, swollen and cold as a block of ice. Straightaway, she sent for a medical doctor who came to the house - in England, doctors actually still visit you - and told her to get him into a hospital immediately. Kath drove him to the nearest hospital, about seven miles due east from where we live. As I was working in America at the time, Kath was left to deal with the nightmare that was just beginning. She called me as soon as Karl was taken to the hospital.

At the hospital, an x-ray indicated that Karl appeared to have a blood clot in his foot. Karl was admitted into a ward and given a blood thinner through an intravenous drip to dissolve the clot.

Unfortunately, it had no effect. In fact, Karl's pain became so intense, he was put on morphine, which was also done intravenously.

For the next 48 hours, the nursing staff continued pumping morphine and blood thinner into his body. On Tuesday morning, it appeared the clot was dissolving. Karl's foot was not as dark as it was when he was first admitted on Sunday. A dye was injected into his legs and more x-rays were made. The new x-rays indicated more blood clots present in his legs. By Tuesday afternoon, the pain and discoloration came back with a vengeance. The pain was now totally unbearable, and the drugs weren't helping.

At this point, the doctor in charge ordered Karl transferred to another hospital about eight miles west of where we live, with better facilities and more up-to-date scanners. Karl was transferred late Tuesday afternoon, and on Wednesday a CAT scan was taken of both his legs. His condition was diagnosed as Peripheral Arteriosclerosis. All of the arteries in his left leg were completely blocked with fatty deposits. Now they weren't sure if it might have been gangrene in his left foot. His right leg was almost as bad. The only option was to amputate.

Kathleen was visiting Karl when the doctors delivered their devastating news - to save Karl's life, both of his legs would have to be removed from the knees down. The left leg would be amputated within the next five days and the right leg the following week.

Kath called me immediately from the hospital. It was late Wednesday evening in England, early afternoon in California. "You have to come home right away," she said. "They can't do anything for Karl. They are going to amputate his left leg on Saturday and take the other next week. What he's got is irreversible."

On Saturday, April 24th, the night before Karl's problem first started, I was in Santa Monica in the final weeks of my healing tour through the USA. That night I woke up from a dream. The dream was really, really realistic, and, at the time, very confusing.

In the dream, I was asked by a man I used to work with if I would go to his son's house and clear out the gutter that collects the rain. His son lives in a row house, where all the homes adjoin, and I go to unblock it. When I climb up the ladder and look in, I see the boy's gutter is completely blocked with gray grunge, but on either side, his neighbors' gutters are completely clear. So, I scoop out all the grunge and dismantle that section of the gutter and bring it down for further inspection. I realize more work has to be done on it, so I take the gutter to a Home Depot and ask people there if they can help me to repair it. End of dream.

On Wednesday I was in San Jose, and in a panic from Kath's call about the forthcoming amputations. Until then the dream meant nothing - but now it began to make sense, and gave me hope. The dream, I thought, is some kind of a message. It's a father and son dream. The blocked gutter could be my son's blocked arteries. Still I was puzzled about why I should be asking other people to try and help me repair the gutter after I cleaned it? I had been sending out remote healing for Karl - in fact it was almost non-stop prayers. Could it be that my dream was trying to tell me I needed the prayers of many people to get him through this crisis?

I picked up the phone and called my friend Robert Krajenke and asked for prayers, not only from him but his wife Lynne and the prayer group he leads at his church. I also called my dear friends Grethe Tedrick in San Francisco, Darlene Bodnar in Denver, Jennifer Kreitzer in San Jose, and several others. My good friend Amara Ward in New York sent Reiki healing remotely to Karl, and during her lunch break, went to a nearby church to light candles to Mother Mary and to Jesus, praying to them for a miracle. Her parents, Audrey and Jim, also prayed for Karl. Word got back to Toni Romano and then somehow the news got on the Internet. People all over America were now praying for my son's recovery, including the Glad Helpers at the A.R.E. in Virginia Beach.

I stepped off the plane in Manchester, England on Friday morning, April 30th at 7:30 a.m. It would be almost 10 a.m. before I arrived home. I lost no time getting to the hospital to see Karl. When Kath and I arrived, Karl was being taken down for another test. A local anesthetic was to be administered so a small tube with a camera inside could be inserted and fed down into his arteries to see if it could tell the surgeon if the problem had worsened or not. They were concerned the condition could go into his heart. I only had time to say, "Hello, how are you doing, son?" before they wheeled him away.

The nurses suggested we come back to be with him in about three hours. Kath and I went home with heavy hearts to wait until we could see him. An hour and a half later, the phone rang. It was Catherine, our youngest daughter. She had gone to the hospital to visit her brother, not knowing he had been taken down for tests. Catherine was clearly very excited.

"They just brought Karl up from the theater. They can't find anything at all wrong with him! They don't know why or how, but he is completely clear. They say he can come home!" Kath put down the phone, and we sat for a few minutes in shocked silence.

I wanted to go to the hospital. I needed to ask some questions. I really wanted to see the surgeon. Don't get me wrong, I was over the moon that Karl was ok, but also I was a bit angry that we were put through 40 hours of agony about having his legs amputated.

The surgeon was not available to see me, so then I collared three nurses who had been looking after Karl and asked the obvious question. "Why was it that less than 48 hours ago my son was told that he would have to have both legs amputated, and now he is completely free from blocked arteries."

Two of the nurses claimed they had never seen anything like it before. What he had was irreversible, they said, amputation was the only thing going for him. "I don't know," one replied calmly. "Sometimes we get to see miracles and I think we just witnessed one today." She smiled a smile that said God had been present with Karl over the last few days. Indeed He/She had. The prayers of all the people praying for a full recovery had been answered.

A few minutes later, I encountered the nurse in charge and asked the same question. "Maybe it was the blood thinning drug that kicked in at the eleventh hour, or it may have been the camera we inserted into him that cleared him out." She was clearly baffled by the almost instant remission.

As I said in the beginning, as a spiritual healer, I have been present to many miracles, great and small. I don't know why, but sometimes, a condition may need more than one person praying for it. Sometimes you have to come together as a group, as a team. If it becomes too emotional, the emotion can block the flow of energy. Maybe, just maybe, that's why my dream was showing me I had to bring other people to help. Now I don't care if it was the camera that was the physical instrument to clear the blockage. The thing is, prayers were asked for, and prayers were answered.

I made phone call after phone call back to the States informing people of Karl's miracle. Everyone was overjoyed with the news. I understand that Amara, the lady who went to church and prayed to Mary and Jesus, returned to the very same church and thanked Mother Mary and her Son for the miracle we were given.

A few days later I was asked the question – "How do you know it was the prayers and not what the medical profession did that brought him back to full health?" My reply was – I don't know. But when the chips were down and the only option was amputation, less than 48 hours later he was totally ok. A few years ago I heard Dannion Brinkley speak in Columbus, Ohio. He spoke about his most recent near death experience. Art Bell, on his radio show, had put out to the nation and to the world that Dannion was close to death. At this talk, Dannion said that he could actually feel the prayers bringing him back; his spirit was wanting to go, but the prayers were bringing him back. Then he actually said, "The next time you hear Dannion Brinkley is close to death, for God's sake don't pray for me. Let me go! I'm telling you, your prayers brought me back!"

Perhaps it was a combination of prayers and medical intervention that brought about my son's miracle. Right now – it does not matter. We have our son back. I thank God for what the medics did and for everyone who prayed for him. God bless you all. I can't thank you enough. You were all part of a team that brought forth a miracle.

Postscript. Karl was discharged from the hospital on Saturday, May 1, 2004 – six days after being admitted – completely free from the blocked arteries.

Karl continued to make good progress from the illness that threatened him with amputation of his legs. The weeks came and went along with his 30th birthday and it seemed his life was back to normal. However, the problem was that his life consisted of him spending almost every day alone in his bedroom playing his video games on his TV. Because of long standing emotional problems he was never able to work. And although he was once assessed as having an IQ of 130 he found it very difficult to communicate with people. Then in October 2004 it appeared that another miracle was in the offing. He expressed a wish that he would like his own place to live. He had been staying with his Mum and me for over three years and now he felt he wanted his own space. Things were looking good.

We managed to find him a very nice two-bedroom apartment about a mile or so from where we live. He wanted a place with two bedrooms so that his 7-year-old daughter Lauren could visit with him on some weekends. Although Karl had been in a relationship some years earlier it did not last, but Lauren's mother, Karen, allowed her to visit our son on a regular basis. The little girl was Karl's pride and joy. She always seemed to lift his spirits. He thought the world of her and she likewise thought the world of him.

As Karl had no income and therefore no savings, it was left to Kathleen and me to furnish and decorate the apartment for him. It took us a while but we managed to get it together for him. Finally on Monday, November 1, 2004 it was moving-in day. "Keep the place tidy Karl, and stay out of trouble." I told him as I left him for his first night stay in his own home.

I gave it a couple of days and then went over to visit with him to see how he was doing. "I've been having nightmares Dad," he told me over a cup of tea. "What kind of nightmares?" I asked. "Someone is trying to kill me and it's so real it's scary." I tried to reassure him that it was because he was living in a house that he was still not used to and that he would be ok in a couple of days when he had gotten used to it.

I decided to call in and see him the following day – Thursday, November 4th. "Anymore nightmares?" I asked. "No, but the heating system isn't working," he informed me. Using my cell phone I called the maintenance department who assured me they would call first thing Friday morning, November 5th. "I'll leave you my phone number," I told them. "Sometimes my son stays in bed till noon. I have a key. Give me a call and I'll come down and let you in."

Sure enough, Friday morning at about 10:30 they phoned and asked if I could go over and let them in. While the two-man heating crew were sorting out what tools to bring in from their work van, I unlocked the door and went into Karl's apartment. "Get yourself up Karl – they've come to fix your heating." No reply. First I checked his bedroom which was empty. Then the second bedroom, but he was not there either. Then I walked into his living room and found Karl laying on the floor – dead. The maintenance men made a hasty retreat. Although numb with shock I was able to call for an ambulance and the police. A post-mortem would later reveal that Karl died from a fatal reaction to the drug heroin. Apparently late Thursday night he came across two local men who persuaded him to try the stuff. It cost him his life.

Although devastated I realized that my son's time on Earth was over. I once read that if we wake up from a night's sleep, then we are still working on our mission. Karl never woke up. I guess his mission had been completed. As parents we always did the best we could for him. We loved him when he was here on Earth and we continue to send out our love to him each day in his new abode in the world of spirit. He will never be forgotten.

The final written words about Karl come from his sister Adele. She had wanted to say them in church during his funeral but was too upset to do so.

My final words to you who are reading this are to never take your life or the life of your loved ones for granted. If you need to say I love you – say it. If you need to say I'm sorry – say it. Life is so fragile. Whatever words of kindness you have to say to someone you love – say them now, today – for there may be no tomorrow in which to do so. God bless you all.

And now I will leave it to Adele to bring closure to Karl's earthly life.

To Karl,

In our childhood, it was so good for me to know you were there.
My first companion and first friend.
I hold a thousand memories of our shared past,
and treasure every one of them.
Others may have seen you different, but I saw you as you are –

as you've always been. You are the brother of my childhood.
How good it was to know you. Your life and mine joined together at the root.
Whatever we've become, however different the paths we've taken, the memories of you will be with me forever.
You will always be close. A very special part of my life.
Thanks a million Brother.
Goodnight and God Bless.

From your loving sister, Adele.

MALCOLM SMITH

**Malcolm Smith travels throughout the United States and keeps
a full schedule of public healing demonstrations
and private sessions.
For information on his schedule, availability and
appointments, please visit his website at
www.malcolmsmithhealer.org**

THE ASSOCIATION FOR RESEARCH
AND ENLIGHTENMENT

For more information about Edgar Cayce and The Association
for Research and Enlightenment, Inc. (A.R.E.), its services and
worldwide programs, call 1-800-333-4499 or visit the website at
http://www.edgarcayce.org.
The A.R.E. is located at 215 67th Street (at Atlantic Blvd.)
Virginia Beach, VA. 23451-2061

THE A.R.E. OF NEW YORK CITY

is located at 241 West 30th Street, 2nd floor, buzz in #102
New York, NY 10001
212-691-7690

*****

ABOUT THE AUTHORS

MALCOLM SMITH

Born and raised in poverty plagued Northern England, Malcolm Smith's incredible healing hands have relieved pain, suffering and disease for thousands of people throughout England and America. Known as 'an ordinary man with an extraordinary gift,' Malcolm quit school at age 15 to work alongside his father in the Yorkshire coal mines. In 1979, at age 33, his life changed forever when, in a chance meeting, a spiritualist medium revealed to him that he had 'healing hands' and would be given proof of this within three days. As predicted, three days later his wife suffered a flare up of a chronic kidney condition which her doctors had pronounced cured. As her agony intensified and with no relief in sight, skeptical but desperate, Malcolm placed his hands on her back and her pain vanished, never to return. Malcolm kept his gift a secret, and for the next two years used it only on his wife and children until a raucous poltergeist forced him to seek help at a local Spiritualist Church where he first learned of Spiritual Healing, and his healing ministry was born.

"Healers don't heal," Malcolm states. "God does the healing." The power that flows through Malcolm's hands has restored sight and hearing, cured cancers and other debilitating diseases. The list of problems presented to him includes virtually every physical, emotional, mental and spiritual condition a person could suffer. While some offer 'the power of suggestion' as the basis for his cures, Malcolm's success with healing animals, tiny babies and comatose accident victims appears to rule out 'suggestion' as an explanation of his success, and implies another force, or energy, is involved.

In this first person account, Malcolm shares his incredible story of personal transformation, healing miracles, soul testing challenges and spirit guidance. "My life has taught me that we are all capable of miracles," Malcolm says. "The power is within us." The life of this 'ordinary man' offers a powerful testimony of the possibility in all our lives.

ROBERT KRAJENKE

Robert Krajenke is the author of *Edgar Cayce's Story of the Old Testament* (3 volumes) and *Spiritual Power Points* (A.R.E. Press). He is an ordained metaphysical minister, a teacher and workshop/ seminar leader. He can be reached at rwk.asaph@cox.net.

*****

CPSIA information can be obtained
at www.ICGtesting.com
Printed in the USA
BVOW03s0143071017
497031BV00001B/39/P